TEACHERS:
YOU CAN'T LIVE WITHOUT THEM

DEAN BURESH

©2022 by Dean Buresh
Cover art and digital design ©2022 Kerry Hilton

All rights reserved.

No part of this book may be reproduced or transmitted in any form or by any electronic or mechanical means, including photocopying, recording, or by any information storage and retrieval system, without the express written permission of the author or publisher, except where permitted by law.

DEDICATION

To my parents, Louis and Elma Buresh, my sister Mary Ann, my wife Gerrie, and my daughters Julie and Karen...

For "putting up with me."

And <u>ALL</u> the teachers in this book—"Thank You!"

CONTENTS

ACKNOWLEDGEMENTS..5
INTRODUCTION..6
CHAPTER 1..7
CHAPTER 2..14
CHAPTER 3..19
CHAPTER 4..27
CHAPTER 5..39
CHAPTER 6..47
CHAPTER 7..58
CHAPTER 8..65
CHAPTER 9..68
CHAPTER 10..74
CHAPTER 11..77
CHAPTER 12..79
CHAPTER 13..81
CHAPTER 14..84
CHAPTER 15..88
CHAPTER 16..91
EPILOGUE...94
MUST READS..95
MY TEACHERS...96
WHAT I HAVE LEARNED...97
ABOUT THE AUTHOR...116

ACKNOWLEDGEMENTS

I would like to thank Dan Haag and Julie Buresh for their knowledgeable input and suggestions for this book. I also owe many thanks to my experienced publisher, Kerry Hilton, for his time and effort in producing it. And, finally, I thank my wife, Gerrie, who encouraged me to undertake this project in the first place and also for her editing and transcribing the copy. Without her, this book would never have happened.

All the proceeds from the sale of the book will be given to the Prairie School Foundation.

INTRODUCTION

This book was inspired by my sister Mary Ann and her husband Bill. They each had written books about their lives, family and journey. Mary Ann did a fantastic job of covering our family, our ancestors, and the tough lives they had as immigrants from Czechoslovakia. She also wrote about her childhood, being a parent and being a teacher. Stop! Both of our parents were teachers, both in one-room schoolhouses! I started kindergarten at Lone Willow School, a one-room schoolhouse outside of Cedar Rapids, Iowa. Mrs. Dee was my teacher.

    My cousin Ernie Buresh also wrote a book called *The Advantages of Growing Up Poor*. (ISBN 9781514211304) Unlike them, my life took a completely different turn. But wait, I'm getting ahead of myself. (By the way, I still miss and long for Iowa!)

1

My Train

This is a book about teachers—yes, primary, secondary, etc. But beyond that, it's about how good you are at listening and learning what people teach you. These teachers come in all shapes and forms. The biggest mistake we make is we oftentimes don't listen to them, and we don't give them enough credit when we learn something. We forget to say "Thank you!" or, my favorite, "Good coach!", implying that you listened to what they said.

A word about thank you notes...since our schools don't teach cursive handwriting anymore, I don't think you can ever hand-print cards and send enough of them by "snail mail." Yes, I'm talking about sitting down and composing a hand-written thank you note and mailing it—not a text, not an e-mail—a thank you to someone who did something for you or your company or organization.

When I've done this, the response to me is amazing because the overwhelming majority of people don't do this, and I am not sure I know why! It is so easy to do. I can count on one hand the number of thank you acknowledgements I've received from associates or clients for tickets, etc., I've gotten for them. In my volunteer work, I've insisted our board members call or write thank you notes to our donors. It's too important not to do so.

Life is like a train ride. You board at the station when you are born with your mother and father and siblings (in my case, an older sister). As your life unfolds, people get on your train. Some stay on, some get off, and some get back on. On your journey, you may encounter an event or a conversation that can dramatically change your ride and the entire course of your life and career. You'll read about my "ride" and how people like Mr. Neuhouse, Dennis, my wife, Bart, Dick, David, Gene, and Julie changed the route I was taking. The key is to be able to recognize these situations and learn from these people. Someone once said to me, "I know what you do. You collect people!"

So, let's begin the ride. I hope you enjoy it. I once had a client kiddingly tell me that I was living proof that anything is possible in America! Hopefully, you'll get some take-aways that will help you continue to grow and develop as a person. Growing—that's the key! So ask yourself, "Did I grow today?" Or "What did I learn today?"

Climb aboard with me and start meeting my collection of teachers and lessons, starting with my parents and sister. Lessons are numbered, and a list of them can be found at the end of this book as well as the names of numerous people who taught me a lot.

I was born in Cedar Rapids, Iowa, and grew up on an acreage where I had the opportunity to raise rabbits, sheep and even several pigs. Not only did the rabbits and pigs provide delicious food for our table, but we were able to sell the wool from the sheep. Being baptized a Catholic, after about fourth grade, I would go every Saturday morning to Catechism class in Cedar Rapids at St. Wenceslaus Church. I learned about Jesus Christ and the Roman Catholic faith. It lasted all morning, and the nuns and priests were very nice. I guess they felt sorry for us "pagan kids" whose parents couldn't afford to send their kids to a parochial school. That's where a nun, Sister Regina Niichel, got on my train and is still on it today. Surprisingly enough, my sister Mary Ann would go on to marry Regina's brother, Bill Niichel. At the time, she was in the back of the train, but over the years, she moved up and now occupies a seat in the first car.

After catechism, I'd walk from St. Wenceslaus to my dad's feed store and ride home with him when he closed at noon. My dad rented out space to a veterinarian, Dr. Paul Brimmer, who got the Wall Street Journal every day and suggested I read it. I did, but didn't understand a word of it. (However, it was a lot more interesting than the Baltimore Catechism!)

Dr. Brimmer mainly treated large animals such as cows and pigs, but he did care for our cocker spaniel, Chips. As busy as he was, he would always take a few minutes to talk with me. His wife Glennys liked me as well and always had time for me. When I reached high school, he asked if I was interested in buying and owning some stock. To be polite, I said yes, not knowing what I was saying or doing. His suggestions were very simple: People will always drink pop and eat junk food (Pepsi and Coke) and will want to live a long time and take medications to stay alive (Merck, Johnson & Johnson and Pfizer). Today we still own Pepsi (Taco Bell stock). We should have kept the drug company stocks, but then again when you're in high school, you think you'll live forever. **See Lesson 1 – Invest with Your Head, Not with Your Heart**

Having no children, in their later years, the Brimmers instituted a charitable foundation which supports local charities in the Cedar Rapids area that focus on feeding and clothing the less fortunate. "Doc" said, "I made all my money from the people in and around Cedar Rapids, and I want it to stay there—no buildings, just money directly to the people." Gerrie and I are honored to serve on the board.

The first person on one's train is obviously one's mother. My wife believes I probably had the perfect childhood—loving parents, a sister, and it didn't hurt being born in the USA and being a white male. **See Lesson 2 – The Railroad Tracks.** We are only now acknowledging as a society and as a country what a huge advantage that is from the beginning of the "ride". It was not until I was in the Army that I realized what racism was and is. More on that later.

My mother worked part-time as a substitute teacher. She never said an unkind word about anyone. Her classic comment was "People are funny!" which could mean any number of things. She <u>never</u> threw anyone "under the bus" for their lifestyle or their behavior. I regret to write that I unfortunately was not able to take after my mother. I believe the first 10 or 12 years of a child's life sets the tone and outcome of their entire life and their relationship with their parents and siblings. You learn the key attributes and values that guide you forever—trust, integrity, honesty, compassion, sympathy, empathy, faith, and especially, gratitude. **(See my Reading List.)**

I guess I was too much like my father. (Incidentally I was born 9 years after my sister, and for the first 8 to 10 years of my life, I thought I was adopted!) He was always there for me in grade school, high school, college and throughout our married life until he was hobbled with a stroke at 92 years of age. Fishing, hunting, Boy Scouts, sports—I could always count on him and he was very patient with me. Yes, he would occasionally raise his voice but he never attacked me personally. I tried to pass this on to our daughters. For example, when one of our daughters would come to me with a problem or question, I asked them what they thought they should do and what their solution was to the problem. Over time, it was amazing how good they became at solving their own problems. If I didn't agree with their solution, I would spend whatever time it took to challenge them until we all agreed what the best solution was. My dad would always ask me after we lost a football game, "What did you learn?" It wasn't about winning. Lessons about winning were self-evident.

Patience with me must have been something he had a lot of. Especially when I was sent home from a camping trip because I put a snake in the sleeping bag of another scout. Surprise, surprise! I never made it to Eagle Scout. Life Scout was as high as I got. There were many great camping trips with our Scoutmasters—great dads who were great role models.

However, much to my father's dismay, things got a little rocky for me when I started driving. Soon after I got my license, I had gotten several tickets and had to go to traffic school. I attended all the sessions but was counted absent at one by mistake. My mom was hosting her Homemakers Club one afternoon, when the sheriff showed up at her door and said, "Mrs. Buresh, I have a warrant for your son's arrest." My mom said, "Sir, there must be some mistake!" He rolled his eyes and replied, "Ma'am, that's what they all say!" At that point, you might say, the train I was on was going through a tunnel. **See Lesson 3 – Kids Should Suffer the Logical Consequences.**

Grandparents, aunts and uncles should never be taken for granted. They can be a terrific source for information and learning. You need to realize I am probably the least mechanical DIY, handy, common-sense person I know when it comes to putting something together and repairing something. Specifically, I don't even know the proper way to hold a hammer and pound a nail. My Uncle Louis, Uncle Joe, and Uncle Walter must have wondered how I was ever going to survive when I was on my own. My Uncle Joe took me fishing, My Uncle Walter made beautiful clocks, and Uncle Louis farmed, and I'm sure all of them were thinking, "I'm not sure what Dean's going to do if he ever grows up."

About sexism—with an older sister, I <u>never</u> felt my mom or dad treated my sister or me differently from one another. They made that very clear on many occasions and, in fact, I was frequently reprimanded if I thought I was better than my older sister. My parents always made it very clear to me that we were equals. My sister was very popular in high school, and some of her male friends wanted to pay me a nickel if I told them every time she went on a date and with whom! I got up to 15 cents before my dad found out. Not pretty! **See Lesson 4 – Equality of the Sexes.**

I was very fortunate to have had two "dads"—my biological one and the one who was our neighbor at the lake in Wisconsin, Don Grant. For over 35 years, I learned more about nature, and especially fishing, on our lake than you could ever imagine. In addition, he had three daughters, and he and his wife Elie were a great sounding board for Gerrie and me with our two daughters. He and Elie had way more wisdom and common sense than Gerrie and me. Like my own father, I still miss him today. I had the honor of delivering a eulogy at his funeral.

2

My Childhood

I cannot emphasize enough as a parent how important it is to spend meaningful time with your children. It's tougher for single parents, but you have to make time. Sure, earning a living is important, but you have such a short time with them up until the 7th or 8th grade. Then the hormones kick in, and they develop hearing disorders. "What?" Listening goes on hold until later.

I was lucky. I had a learning disability before techniques, testing, and even medications were available. I was terrible at spelling and still am. Teachers would say, "Sound it out!" Hell, that didn't help a bit!

I have a terrible time with numbers spoken aloud but no problem with written numbers. The only thing that saved me was my mother. In grade school and high school, she spent numerous evenings and weekends tutoring me on mathematics, spelling and reading. Many of these sessions would end up with us both crying. **See Lesson 5 – If Your School Isn't Doing a Good Job, Change Schools.**

As a parent, take the time to understand if your child is struggling in school. Today I worry that some parents blame the teachers for their children's problems. I know it's difficult to acknowledge that your child needs help but do so. Because if not recognized early, it is a tremendous disadvantage to the child later in life. The good news, I think, as a society, we are getting better at recognizing these problems. Mine plagued me through college and graduate school, and even later in my career—after flunking Algebra in 9th grade and Statistics in college.

More on my father…I learned the value of working at an early age by helping him do things around the house. One of his favorite lines was "No one ever died from hard work." He would also say, "Never ask someone to do something you wouldn't or couldn't do yourself." I am sure if he were alive today, he would say, "The only place where the word 'success' comes before 'work' is in the dictionary." **See Lesson 6 – Never Ask Someone to Do Something You Couldn't Do Yourself.**

Let's talk about the value of money as it relates to work, which leads me to my first job. In 1962 the principal and superintendent of our high school decided that the best way to keep our school buildings in tip-top shape was to have all the athletes do the janitorial work on a daily basis before classes started. Yes, that meant we would be at school by 7:00 a.m., do our jobs, and be done by 8:30 in time for class. For that I was paid $1.50 for an hour-and-a-half of work! Let me tell you, the schools were spotless! If an athlete saw someone making a mess or destroying property, it would never happen a second time! Even in the elementary school, the word spread pretty quickly that if you did something, someone would report it to their "big brother." Problem solved!! Did I like cleaning the girls' bathroom? No! We did rotate duties, thank God. So once a month I would receive a check for $30 or so. I was rich!

Which leads me to my next lesson on the value of money. My parents wanted a new TV for the kitchen. So, my father and I went to Montgomery Ward, our "Walmart," so to speak, in Cedar Rapids. We found one for $500. That was the posted price. My dad asked the salesperson if that was their best price. He said, "Let me check with my boss." He was back in less than 5 minutes and said, "I can let you have it for $450." My dad said, "We'll take it!" As we left the store with the new TV, my dad said, "You were uncomfortable when I asked the salesman about getting a discount, weren't you?" I said, "Yes." He replied, "How long would it have taken you to save $50?" I said, "A month." He smiled and said, "It took us 5 minutes!" OK, it's not as easy as it used to be to do and have these kinds of negotiations, but it never hurts to ask in certain situations.

In 1970 Gerrie and I had just moved to Chicago from my parents' house after getting out of the Army. No job, no prospects for one. So interviewing was about to start. I came out of the bedroom with a green plaid double-knit suit I bought at the Army post exchange. My dad had not left for work yet. In a very relaxed and tactful manner, he said "I think you will look better in one of my suits." I went on my first interview in a conservative blue pinstripe, right out of "Dress for Success!"

Again, I am getting ahead of myself. It's time to stop the train and pick up some of my formal teachers whom I would like you to meet. First on the teacher train of College Community Schools was Mrs. Dee. Remember her? She was my kindergarten teacher at Lone Willow School. She now was my First Grade teacher at College Community School. How lucky was that! Now I'm going to a brand new school and riding a school bus. We got hot lunch—no more cold sandwiches. I was just like the city kids now even though I lived in the country.

My sister may have been "pissed" when I was born. She was 9 years old, and all-of-a-sudden her whole world changed as I was the only boy on both sides of the family. All my cousins are girls. But I never sensed any jealousy. She was always there for me. Even today we talk once a week. I was always in awe of her, respected her, thought she was beautiful and clearly more intelligent than I was. So, I grew up in a family where boys and girls were treated equally, and I respected that. I think that is why I never had any problem working with women and, more importantly, hiring and promoting female managers. **See Lesson 7 – Always Hire People Who are Smarter than You Are.**

All of my aunts and uncles and extended family played a key role in my growing up but my favorite uncle was Great Uncle Smokey. He was a World War I veteran, a doughboy, who lived in a house with no electricity until he, my dad and Uncle Joe did the wiring for it. I can't imagine what he would have thought of the internet on which we depend so heavily today. He always gave me a Pepsi when I came to visit him.

Uncle Joe always took me fishing and hunting. It was in his company that I had my first and only experience with Copenhagen chewing tobacco. I was helping him bale hay on a hot summer day. He offered me a plug but never told me to spit, so I swallowed it and felt sick the rest of the day. Since then tobacco and I never got along.

Before I go off to school, I want you to think about your family and your parents and how they shaped your life—the activities, the conversations, the disagreements, the spankings (yes, the discipline!) I had my share of issues, but that extended family was always there 24/7. I just wish everyone had that luxury. And I never once said "Thank You" to them for being there. Before you read any further, write those family members a Thank You note, or call them before it's too late.

3

Grade School and High School

Grades 1, 2, 3, and 4 were a rush against time as a kid—some of the best times of my life. The teachers were terrific. (I mean it!) They cared about me and all of my classmates. They were dedicated professionals who gave it their all every day. And even with my learning handicaps, they spent time with me so I wouldn't fall behind. Those first few grades are so important because that's when you learn the basics like reading, writing and arithmetic and how to interact with people in authority who are not your parents. You learn to listen to instructions, starting with "color between the lines," and respect those same people. Easy for me to say now, but the fact of the matter is I was not a good student.

When my train reached junior high, it was starting to go off the tracks—not de-railing but starting to come close. The teachers were still terrific. As hard as they tried to get me to practice my writing skills and improve my reading during the summer, I didn't. I would much rather hang out with my neighborhood friends. That was a lot more fun than schoolwork. I got mostly C's in grade school with comments such as "Settle down, young man, and work a little harder!" even from the Superintendent of Schools at the time.

Even though I started playing a trumpet in the band and eventually a French horn in the high school marching band, my heart was never in playing a musical instrument. Football became my passion, but more on that later. However, Steve Bures (different spelling from my last name) and I were able to cause somewhat of a disturbance one morning before band had started. All the "bandies" would come to school with their instruments and leave them in the Music Room before their 1st Period classes. In those days, no one locked up their instruments in the carrying cases because they were "safe" in the Music Room. Steve and I thought it would be great fun to lock everyone's instrument cases and leave all the keys in a big pile on the band teacher's desk. There were about 35 students in the band. As you can imagine, when it came time for band practice to begin, chaos erupted. Of course, no one knew which keys belonged to which cases! Even at the end of 1st Period, there were still many instrument cases that remained locked. And so, the final chapter is written in my marching band career!

My sister was at Iowa State University, and we would visit her occasionally on weekends. I thought living away from home like she did was pretty cool! But I figured that would never happen to me because I wasn't "college material."

Soon I was a freshman at Prairie High School, and we moved about 8 miles away to the town of Fairfax. My parents built a beautiful home, but I missed my friends from the old neighborhood. I was playing in the band and had started my football career. My grades began to slip from B's to C's and D's. My mom was now a substitute teacher in the high school, so I can only imagine the grief she was going through in the Teachers' Lounge hearing things like, "Well today Dean threw a fork in the lunchroom garbage disposal when he was clearing off his tray, completely shutting it down!"

About football and sports in general, get your kids into something. We didn't have golf or tennis, but those sports carry over easily later in life. Participation in sports teaches you about getting along with others and working together. I had just finished my freshman year, and my mom was still substitute teaching. After school I was waiting for my mom outside in the hall when I overheard her talking to Mr. Boubin, the football coach. She asked him, "How did Dean do this season?" He said, "Elma, Dean is a fine boy, but he is not going to be a great player. He is just too nice!"

I can remember that conversation like it happened yesterday. It was like a switch just flipped in my brain. "Too nice!!!! Well, we will just see about that!!!" I started running and working out that spring and summer. I showed up for practice in the fall like a changed person. I was going to show the coaches what "too nice" was really like. As a result, I made the varsity team, one of two sophomores, and lettered, playing defensive guard and defensive end. My grades started to improve in a short period of time. I got a few B's and my self-esteem started to improve. At the beginning of my junior year, as football season was just starting, we won our first game. My family, and even my sister and brother-in-law were coming to all my games.

In 1963, my junior year, the Minneapolis Vikings and Chicago Bears played an exhibition game at Memorial Stadium—a really big deal for Cedar Rapidites! (I had played there, and our team, The Prairie Hawks, had gotten run over by Cedar Rapids Jefferson and Regis High Schools. They were better than we were.) Somehow our coach got a few of us into the Viking's locker room at half time to hear their coach talk about what they had to do to win in the second half. But what I remember most had nothing to do with Norm Van Brocklin, the coach, giving a motivational speech or the plays and diagrams on the blackboard. What struck me was everyone was smoking cigarettes! I mean every coach and every player! You could barely see any of them. I was shocked! I never took up smoking but a number of my high school friends did. I often wonder now what our coaches thought about that visit in hindsight because all they ever predicted was that cigarettes would stunt your growth.

So, following our first win, we had a light week of workouts. But on Thursday's practice before Friday-night's game, we practiced against the second-string team. I was playing defensive end, and they were going to run one more play directed at my side of the line. They double teamed me and knocked me down. Then I got kicked in the right kidney. The next thing I knew they were taking me to Mercy Hospital and my season was over.

I was devastated and depressed and couldn't believe what had just happened. I wanted to play football and be with all the jocks in school, but where was I? In the hospital. I was there for a week—young enough, no permanent damage, but I wouldn't be able to play again until I was a senior. I totally lost interest in football, didn't go to the games, didn't care how the team was doing, and my grades started to slip again. I worked in the morning at school before class, but rode the bus home after school and couldn't care less about anything.

Then—Mr. Ken Marsh, the science teacher who taught Physics, wanted to talk to me. I was taking Chemistry at the time and getting D's. Mr. Marsh, one of the more colorful people to get on my train, was big and had worked as a stunt man for Tarzan in Hollywood. Every athlete I knew was afraid of him. In fact, one time some kids from Jefferson High School came out to Prairie when school was letting out. They wanted to pick up some of the Prairie girls. I can remember how Mr. Marsh pulled the two guys out of their car simultaneously through the car window, one in each arm, and asked them if he could help them! We never had another problem with anyone from Cedar Rapids coming out to pick up Prairie girls again.

So why did he want to see me? I wasn't taking Physics until next year. Granted, we had almost set a substitute teacher on fire with a Bunsen burner, but he didn't know about that. So, after 6th Period, I went to his office and I was scared! He wore a patch over one eye, wore a hearing aid, and ran the Science Club. I was a member of the Science Club because we were building rockets, and gun powder was involved. Naturally I was all in! That's where my best friend, Dennis Faltis, lost his hand in an explosion from one of our "projects" gone bad. Dennis ended up playing a very critical part on my train ride, but more on that later.

Mr. Marsh said to me, "I want you to start working for me after school repairing and taking care of all the audio-visual equipment we have plus the copying machines." I was now going to get a raise! That meant I could drive the Drivers Training car around to the elementary and junior high buildings and pick up the machines and then deliver them after they were fixed. What's the catch? "If you're ever going to make it to the 12th grade, you better start 'shaping up!'"—his words. I will never forget that conversation. Talk about a dream job! I was on top of the world!

My senior year rolled around, and I was still getting C's, but no more D's. Besides that, I was elected president of the student council and, yes, I was dating the Homecoming Queen! Along with Lon Scriven, I was selected to be a co-captain of the football team. This was going to be a great year! I was getting A's in several courses, but I was still struggling in English and Spanish. The C's kept coming in those two areas. At that time, I was convinced there were always going to be teachers who just plain didn't like me. I guess that is only normal when you're a senior in high school, which I now realize simply wasn't true. Later, my Spanish would ultimately result in my saving a couple of soldiers' lives in the Army, and my public speaking and English debate experience would result in my winning a partial scholarship to the University of Iowa and the American Legion speaking competition at Prairie High School.

I was now in Mr. Marsh's Physics class and received B's from him. He would often kid me saying, "You have an inferiority complex because you are inferior!" And then he would smile and laugh. Because he was always in demand outside of school as a speaker, he told me one day that I was going to speak to the Fairfax American Legion celebration. I was in shock! He said, "The Veterans need to hear from some of our youth." I can't tell you how proud I was, and I rehearsed that speech with my parents until I am sure they knew it better than I did. Yes, he was there and heard my speech and said I did a good job. Coming from him, that was the ultimate compliment. I can't remember what I said in the speech, but I am sure it had something to do with how proud I was to be an American. As my senior year came to an end, Mr. Marsh stepped off my train. He obviously had other students he needed to mentor, but I never forgot him for the time he spent with me. **See Lesson 8 – Teachers Can Be Game Changers.**

I remember in one of the final Physics classes of the year, Mr. Marsh said, "This coming week you'll be meeting with Mr. Franklin, the guidance counselor. You'll get your ACT scores, and the day will go like this: Your parents will tell you to get up that morning and go to school. You'll get on the bus. The driver will tell you to sit down and shut up. You'll get to school, get off the bus, and go to your Home Room. Mr. Shirley will tell you to sit down and don't talk until the bell rings. That will signal you to go to your first class, where when your name is called, you will see Mr. Franklin and he will ask you, 'So what do you want to do with the rest of your life after you graduate in a few weeks?'"

<u>What</u>, <u>what</u>? Already I wasn't looking forward to walking into Mr. Franklin's office for the "guidance counseling session" because I'd convinced myself I was not college material. Hey, I scored a 14 on my ACT test so I barely ranked in the upper half of my senior class. The bottom half had more common sense than the upper half, and they were going to be just fine in life. I, on the other hand, didn't fit with either half. Sure, I had a lot of friends, but I never felt I was accepted by either group.

As graduation approached, I was scared, not knowing what came next. I could feel my train coming to a slow stop. Everyone was getting off, and I don't think I ever felt more alone than those last few weeks of my senior year. Graduation was a blur. I think a Chicago police chief was our commencement speaker. Even as I departed high school, law enforcement was still on my train.

4

Off to the University and Military Service

Somehow, I was accepted at the University of Iowa for admission (state law, I think) to start in the Fall of 1964. My job at the high school with Mr. Marsh was over, and I had no prospects for a job that summer. My mom suggested I go to summer school at Iowa and get a head start on the other freshmen. She suggested I take Rhetoric and Earth Science for 8 weeks, and then I would be ready for the fall semester. It made sense. I had a single room in the Quadrangle, a men's dormitory (no longer in existence), so I was all set. Off I went, about to take some more passengers onto my train.

It was time to register for my first class, which was going to be Rhetoric. I got in line at the Rhetoric registration table. (In those days, it was all done by hand on computer punch cards.) At last, I was greeted by a teaching assistant whose job it was to ask you for your high school grades and ACT scores to determine what level and section would be appropriate. In a matter of less than 30 seconds, he said, and I will never forget these words, "What are you doing here? You're just wasting your parents' money!"

I guess that score of 14 on my ACT was a pretty good indicator of how well I was going to succeed. All I could think was, "Wait a minute, Mr. Graduate Student, you don't know me! You just lit a fire in my brain!" It brought back memories of Mr. Boubin saying I was too nice to play football. I thought, "Well, screw you! I can do this, and I hope our paths cross again at some point in the future!" But they never did in my 5 ½ years as an undergraduate and graduate student.

A few weeks later, I was off to my first Rhetoric class, and I was scared to death, worrying if I could keep up with all the other students. The instructor was a full professor, Archibald Coolidge, teaching an 8-week summer session. Unbelievable! Full professors didn't usually teach summer courses. Here we were, about 20 of us, in Schaeffer Hall. Sitting next to me was John Conzemius, who would have an impact on my entire life and still is on my train to this day. This was his third attempt to complete a college degree, and he was bound and determined this time to see it through. John and I ended up being roommates for two years at Iowa. **See Lesson 9 – Choose Your Roommates. Don't Let Your Roommates Choose You.**

As I was finishing my freshman year in the spring of 1965, I wasn't sure what I was going to major in and had no prospects for a summer job. I had purchased a car, but that had turned into more of a problem than I had imagined. I had to park it about a mile from the dormitory and didn't use it because I was too busy studying. I was in the College of Liberal Arts and had to fulfill my foreign language requirement. John suggested selling the car and going to summer school at the University of Guadalajara, Mexico. Voila! Spanish requirement satisfied, live with a Mexican family, and have a wonderful summer. My parents thought it was a good idea because they knew I would have to sell the car. It was a beauty—a 1965 Chevrolet Impala, 2-door, 327, 250 HP white with red interior. A real chick magnet!! I had to sell it because my parents were not going to pay for the Mexico junket, no matter how hard I tried to sell them on the idea.

So off I went in June by Greyhound bus with a ticket to Mexico City and Guadalajara, where I met up with my friend John. We lived with a couple who were both professors at their city university. She was Mexican and he was German. He arrived from Germany immediately after the end of World War II, perhaps by landing secretly on the beach in Acapulco after dark? They had no children, and they both spoke English, Spanish and German. They told us if we were going to learn Spanish, we would have to speak it all the time, and that's what motivated me to become fluent in Spanish that summer. I couldn't believe it, I even dreamed in Spanish when I was there! **See Lesson 10 – Immerse Yourself.**

Back at Iowa, in the fall of my sophomore year, I had to declare a major, but I had just had a great summer and had this "college thing" all figured out. The reason I was going to major in Rhetoric, Logic and

Public Address is because I was still struggling with my writing. Therefore, I knew I didn't want to be a newspaper writer, and I knew I couldn't handle all the math required for the business school. I was going to stay in Liberal Arts and become a Speech and Dramatic Arts teacher.

I was also in Army ROTC during college. This was during the Viet Nam war, and ROTC was one way to avoid the draft. I joined the Pershing Rifles, the Army drill team, where I met Ron Boe, who is still on my train today. He was a couple years ahead of me, and I was intimidated by him. But he had a car and lived off-campus, and I was hoping I too would someday have a car again.

The train ride was getting a little bumpy the second semester of my sophomore year. I was working part time in the Dormitory Office sorting mail, taking in dry cleaning, selling tickets to various University events and being a disk jockey on the dormitory radio station. "Doug Jones" was my radio name, and college classes—well, they weren't a priority like they used to be. In those days, parents got copies of all your grades, and I'll never forget the phone call from my dad, saying, "You're flunking Psychology??? What's going on???" My response, which sounded good at the time was, "Those are only mid-term grades. The teachers just do that to get you to study harder the last half of the semester."

Well, guess what? My parents weren't buying it. I was told in no uncertain terms that this summer I wasn't going on a junket. I would be getting a job. But I'd been selected to be a Dormitory Hall Floor Resident Advisor beginning in the fall, so that would cover room and board for my junior year. I'm sure I was hired because I'd worked in the office the year before and they liked me. Lord knows it wasn't based on academics. If they would have checked my academic records, I am convinced I would still be rooming with John.

Since I wouldn't be taking any summer courses, my father told me to talk to our next-door neighbor, Mr. Neuhouse, about working at Wilson Foods in Cedar Rapids, a large meat processing plant. They were always looking for people and the pay was great. Mr. Neuhouse was in charge of sales, and I thought, "Wow! I'm going to be working in sales on my way up into management!" He said, "Come on down to the employment office Monday afternoon around 3:00, and we'll get you started." I'm thinking,"I guess I'll be going around getting the mail, cleaning up and getting oriented for Tuesday starting at 8:00." He said don't wear any good clothes. That should have been my first clue.

When I arrive, I'm the only one dressed in jeans, but, OK. And I'm the youngest by far. So, I fill out all the paperwork and wait for my name to be called. Then it happened—words I will never forget. "Buresh—hog kill!" "What??!! There must be some mistake," I thought. Before I had a chance to ask any questions, I was in the plant and I was officially on "Second Shift Hog Kill." I could barely see the office building across the yard from the plant. Well, I didn't have any choice. I was a packing house worker from 3:00 to 11:00 pm, Monday through Friday. **See Lesson 11 – Never Think You Are Better Than Someone Else.**

When I returned to school that fall, I was a junior

and a hall advisor in Quadrangle, the men's dormitory. I realized I needed to start taking courses in my major and get serious about life in general. But, hey, now I had a car again and was free to move about on weekends. Also, I found most of my courses in Speech and Dramatic Arts to be not very difficult. Teaching might just be for me. I had some elective credits to take, so, hey, why not take a Spanish literature class. I could speak it and read it. Besides, chances are I would be the only male in the class. Great place to meet chicks!

So off I go to the English & Philosophy Building for Spanish Literature 101 with my ash tray. Yes, I was smoking Lucky Strikes on occasion. But, hey, you could now smoke in class, so why not in this class? I couldn't smoke in any of my major course classes in Jessup Hall. But here I could, and besides, it was cool—to be smoking, that is.

One of the dormitory hall advisors wanted to line me up for a blind date. I had never been on one before. I was very skeptical. Besides this particular date lived off campus, not in the dorm or sorority house, which sounded like trouble. I'm not sure why I felt that way, but skepticism was running rampant in my brain. I drove to her address. It was in a residential neighborhood so skepticism mounted. I knocked on the door, and to the door came a girl in a Yale sweatshirt. Worst of all was that she was in my Spanish literature class, sat in the back row and didn't talk! Major problem—never date someone in a class you are taking! (In my first summer school Rhetoric class, we had a girl get married and divorced in an 8-week session!) We agreed to have a Coke date with my friend

Max and his date. That led to a disastrous first date to an Iowa basketball game. But after that first date, things just clicked and the rest is history. Fifty-four years later we are still together. Everyone asks, "Are you happily married?" to which I answer, "Of course!" Now I was dating someone I really liked. She was sitting in the seat right behind me on my train with my friends, John and Dennis. I was still in front with my parents and my sister and her family. All good!

Gerrie was a great student and in fact probably inspired me to study more and get some really good grades. Yes, A's and B's! I had climbed out of the "C class" and was really doing well. Gerrie had moved to the women's dorm since she had been living with her brother off-campus and he graduated from law school and left town. As a residence hall advisor, I had a reserved parking place for my 1965 red Chevelle Super Sport. As the year wore on, we had some great times together—going to movies, "woodsies," and eating pizza on Sunday nights when no food was served in the dorms. In case you are wondering, "woodsies" involved alcohol, a campfire and young adults. The rest is left up to your imagination. I was fortunate enough to have an uncle who owned a nearby farm with woods and a pond who kindly hosted these weekly affairs!

Free room and board was one of the best perks for a Residence Hall Advisor like me. Other than making sure the residents didn't burn down the dorm, it was a cushy job. Men didn't have a curfew, and women were not allowed in any of the residents' rooms. Once a month on the weekend, I would be on "Hall Duty" in case of an emergency.

The only emergency I had on Hall Duty occurred on a weekend in January when I was patrolling one of the halls around midnight. I met a resident in a swimsuit headed to the showers. "Strange!" I thought to myself, so I followed him. When I got to the showers, the entrance was blocked with a large piece of plywood covered in plastic. The shower had been turned into a 5-to-6-foot deep swimming pool with several men paddling around having a big time! I had to ask them to drain the "pool" immediately. Other than a few "panty raids" the men attempted on the women's dorms each Spring, it was a great job!

Summer of 1967 came, and I was off to a 6-week summer camp at Ft. Riley, Kansas, part of my ROTC training, with my friend Max and several others. It was a great experience for me. It did a great deal to boost my self-esteem and make me ponder a career in the military. Viet Nam was in the news, with mounting casualties and body counts dominating everything. Our summer camp focused on what we were expected to do when we graduated. The demand for 2nd Lieutenants exceeded the supply.

As I entered my senior year, I was not convinced I wanted to be a teacher. Gerrie was a junior now, and I told her that I loved her and that when I graduated, I wanted to get married. I was made Head Resident of Rienow Hall at the end of the first semester. Fred Bertschinger was one of my hall advisors and challenged me with some of my first management experiences! I was now well into my major but realizing if I were going to teach, I needed a Master's Degree. I saw how much Gerrie was enjoying her courses and believed teaching was for me. But first I had to defer my Army commitment. So, I applied and was deferred for 18 months, which surprised me. Now I needed to get admitted to graduate school, and it was in that process that Professor Ehninger agreed to be my sponsor. One day he told me, "No one in the department can read your handwriting! You need to start printing. Fuzzy on paper, fuzzy up here!" pointing to his head. I've been printing everything ever since.

I graduated in June of 1968 with a B.A. in Rhetoric and Logic and was commissioned a 2nd Lieutenant in the U.S. Army Infantry. Gerrie and I married in September and moved into married student housing. Gerrie finished her studies and graduated in January 1969. I had not applied for the Ph.D. program because I wasn't sure that's what I wanted to do. Also, I still had my military obligation and hadn't decided if a career in the Army might be a good option as well. I would be getting my Master's degree in December of 1970. I wanted to finish up and get my military service behind me as soon as possible and determine if a career in the Army was a next move or a return to graduate school for a Ph.D.

At a family gathering during that time, I spoke with my cousin Lester, who had been a B-17 pilot flying over Germany during World War II. He approached me and said, "I can tell you're worried about going to Viet Nam. I, of course, said, "Yes." He made a suggestion which I have never forgotten and have used throughout my business career. He said, "Keep a pad of paper and a pencil next to your bed, and when you can't sleep or are worried about something, write it down. Chances are what you worried about didn't happen." Boy, was he right! Over the years, that proved to be the case in most instances in everything from a family problem to a client situation. It seems the things that you <u>didn't</u> worry about were always the situations that turned into problems.

I'll never forget in November before graduation, I went to the ROTC office at Iowa to determine where I would begin to attend the Officer Basic Course in the Infantry. Surprisingly, I was told I would not be going into the Infantry but had been transferred to the Adjutant General Corp. The Adjutant General Corp is the administrative branch of the Army, consisting mostly of desk jobs. Their unofficial motto is, "We don't retreat. We backspace!" The Sergeant Major in the office said my assignment was probably because of my proficiency in Spanish. There was a need for junior officers at the training bases who could speak Spanish. I would be going to Ft. Jackson, South Carolina. When I left his office, I knew I wasn't going to make the Army my career. If I could not be in a combat arm branch (Infantry, Armor or Artillery), I knew my chances for advancement were not that good. There was no overturning that decision. Uncle Sam had spoken, end of discussion.

So it's off to the Adjutant General School in Indianapolis for nine weeks in February 1970 and then on to Columbia, South Carolina. In South Carolina, we had a beautiful apartment overlooking an athletic field. Gerrie got a job as a secretary for an insurance company, and I was initially assigned to the Transfer Station, a facility for soldiers completing basic and AIT training who are headed to Viet Nam or Germany. No Spanish so far, but then everything changed. I was reassigned to the Personnel Center, where we were the first soldiers to see draftees and enlistees arrive on the buses and the last soldiers to see them when they retired or got discharged to go home. Although I was at Ft. Jackson for only eighteen months, it had an incredible impact on me. I was dealing with hardship discharges and medical issues, not to mention rescuing two Puerto Ricans from a burning barracks when I was the "Duty Officer" for the evening. The officers and enlisted men I dealt with were some of the most dedicated, honest and hard-working individuals I had ever met. Sergeant Pickup, his wife and kids would have us over dinner. I developed a very strong bond with several of the enlisted sergeants and another lieutenant, Pat Dutcher, who boarded my train and is still on it today. He and his wife, Mary Ann, are godparents to our older daughter.

My first exposure to overt racism came while living in Columbia at that time. I remember shopping in a major department store there and realizing that there was a front entrance for whites and a back entrance for people of color. But racism really came home to me several weeks later when we had a number of Captains and Lieutenants over for dinner. I suggested we all go downtown after dinner and hit the clubs rather than going to the Officers Club at Ft. Jackson, as Gerrie and I usually did. A steak at the Officer's Club was only $1.35, and Canadian Club on the rocks was only 15 cents. The group suddenly went quiet, and finally Ed Moses, a captain, said, "Dean, we can't go to any of those downtown bars. We're Black!" All of a sudden, I felt their pain. These were men and women who had survived Viet Nam, some of them on one or two 12-month tours. And, according to the nightly news, we were burying 100, 200, sometimes 300 soldiers a week.

Every morning I would go into headquarters before 7:00 a.m. and wait for the teletype to start up with the list of Viet Nam casualties from the past 24 hours in our 3rd Army area and whose families would have to be notified that their son or daughter had been killed. A captain or above was assigned that duty. In those days, everyone in the neighborhood knew whose kid was in Viet Nam, so when the green Army Torino pulled up in front of a person's house, people knew it wasn't good news. See **Lesson 12 – Having a Bad Day?**

In the spring of 1971, we were notified that I would be given an early discharge from the Army in November, right before Thanksgiving. I would not be going to Viet Nam because the U.S. was starting to draw down the number of service people there and all over the rest of the world. We were so excited! We couldn't believe this was happening!

5

Discharge from the Army and Where Now?

I can very distinctly remember the evening Gerrie and I found out about my early release from the Army. We were sitting around quietly watching M.A.S.H. when a fellow soldier from my Officer Basic class called and broke the news. After I hung up, I asked myself, "What next?" I guess we go back to Iowa and start looking for a job, or—wait a minute—maybe I should go back and get that Ph.D! Yes! Purdue had a great program in Organizational Communication. I applied. Quite a process! I had to contact my former professors for recommendations and fill out and send an application. Then we waited for a response. It wasn't until late fall that I found out I had been accepted for Fall of 1972. I was so excited I couldn't believe it!

That's when my wife brought our train to a complete halt. She said, "Do you really want to be a college professor?" I said, "I think so." She continued to press the issue by questioning my motives and reasons. She didn't feel that academia was the right environment for someone with my drive. After much discussion, I said, "Let's just go home and think about this." I can't tell you how happy we were to be back in Iowa staying with my parents in Fairfax. The holidays, the family—re-connecting was great!

I had worked part-time for Wilson's meat packing plant on the hog kill and as a fill-in for vacationing salesmen prior to going on active duty. So, I went back to see Mr. Neuhouse for a full-time permanent sales position. Gerrie and I were willing to relocate anywhere. In fact, I had graduated from their sales training program, No. 2 in the class! This time Mr. Neuhouse didn't have any openings for salesmen and suggested I consider other fields besides selling meat. He was very blunt about telling me they would probably be eliminating car route salesmen. Everything would eventually be done by computer—ordering, claims, etc. I remember driving back to Fairfax wondering what now? The Holidays were over, I had no job and no prospects.

Then I heard about a firm called Lendman and Associates from Ron Boe, my old Pershing Rifle Drill Team commander. He told me they were a job placement firm that specialized in finding Fortune 500 jobs for military officers who had finished their tours of duty. They held career weekends in major cities all over the U.S. Ron lived in suburban Chicago and asked me and Gerrie to visit him and go to one of these weekends. Off we went not knowing what to expect. It was a job fair held at the Marriott O'Hare. Companies like GM, IBM, Merck, Ford, Pfizer, Baxter Labs, Redman Industries (the list goes on and on) were participating. Ron told me he got several offers and was hired by Pullman, the manufacturer of railroad cars. The best part was all fees were paid by the employer. Wow!

Job seekers would walk into the ballroom on a Friday night with 300 to 400 other junior officers and line up at tables with the company names you were interested in. If they had suitable positions available, you would leave your resume. If they liked your resume, you might get an interview. This was just too good to be true! I must have handed out 10 to 15 copies of my resume. The next step was to go home and wait for the mail and the phone to ring.

It didn't take long. Pfizer, Procter & Gamble, and Baxter Laboratories all wanted me to return to Chicago and Cincinnati for interviews. Also, Lendman & Associates, who put on these job fairs, wanted to talk to me as well. I couldn't believe it! Back to Chicago I went. I met Steve Lendman and was offered a position as a recruiter for them. It would involve travel to military bases all over the Midwest by plane or in a company car, a 1972 Plymouth Barracuda!

I thought this was perfect because I had no idea what I really wanted to do, plus I could spend time on the career weekends with the company recruiters getting the inside story on all of these Fortune 500 companies. Besides, I got turned down by Pfizer (more on that later). I knew how the military worked. I worked in the Personnel Center at Ft. Jackson while all the soldiers were discharged and knew how to appeal to those folks to get the names of officers who were getting out. Also, I had a great deal of success convincing these young officers to travel to the career weekends all over the U.S.

One minor problem—I was never home in our apartment in Chicago. I traveled five days a week and every-other weekend, I was off to a job fair, working set-up and registration on Friday and Saturday. Then home Sunday morning and departing either Sunday evening or Monday morning for another midwestern military base.

Then it happened. A major change was about to take place at a career weekend at the O'Hare Marriott. I was busy registering attendees, and my friend Dennis (from our rocket-building days in high school who now worked for an advertising agency) and Gerrie were having a drink at the hotel bar, talking about how I was never home anymore. He asked Gerrie if she thought I might like to get into the advertising business working for an agency called Sperry Boom. Dennis was the Media Director and was looking for someone to be a media assistant or a media buyer and he/she wouldn't have to travel. I think that's what appealed to Gerrie—no more travel and home every night.

After the weekend, Dennis set up an interview at their offices near O'Hare Airport. I met with their CEO and senior vice president as well as the associate media director, a woman to whom I would report. This was going to be a change—no longer being independent <u>and</u> reporting to a woman! I was offered the job with an annual salary of $9,600 less than I had made as a lieutenant in the Army or at Lendman!

Moreover, Gerrie was hired by Pfizer and was making $12,000 a year! I took the job and kept asking myself, "Have I made the right decision?" In hindsight it was clear to me that I was hired solely on Dennis's recommendation. I had never taken an advertising course, and I was totally not familiar with how the business worked.

My office consisted of five or six file cabinets, a desk and a chair in a room off the main hall. It was so small, if you wanted to change your mind about something, you would have to step outside, change your mind and come back in. I started sending solicitation letters to DuKane audiovisual dealers for their Yellow Pages co-op program and following up with a phone call. I was so successful, DuKane requested that I stop soliciting dealers. They hadn't budgeted for this much participation. Remember that in high school I had repaired these machines so I could speak their language. I had a ball!

I was given the opportunity to start planning and buying trade/business-to-business media for Sperry Boom's clients, so I was now meeting with media representatives on a regular basis and listening to and asking questions about their publications and the benefits for our clients. My generation was actually post-"Mad Men," but we still had the three-martini lunches and expensive dinners in some of Chicago's finest restaurants all on the pretense of discussing what magazine would meet our clients' needs. In fact, when our older daughter was in first grade, each student was to tell the class what their father did for a living. She said, "He goes out to lunch" because every night when I came home, Gerrie asked, "Where did you go to lunch today?"

The CEO and Dennis decided that I should go into account work, calling on clients and selling the media and creative work our clients asked us to do. I was a bit scared, to be honest. I now had to get input from the clients on what they wanted, come back to the agency, write a creative brief for the writers and art directors, take the finished product back to the client and sell it. I learned very quickly advertising is a tough business. You rise and fall by the strength of your ideas and how well you can sell those ideas and then, most importantly, do they work? My favorite line at the time was, "I hope we come up with something that works before you run out of money!" Most clients didn't think that was all that funny.

Every account executive worries about the client firing him or her and losing the business for the agency. It's like living every day with a big water balloon over your head and the danger of getting wet at any moment because you "screwed up" or "things just weren't working so we're going to make a change." I was very fortunate in my career because that very seldom happened to me. In fact, I've had clients follow me from agency to agency as my career unfolded. Why? The reason, as Dan Gahlon, head of communications for 3M, said to me one time, "Dean, you always do what you think is right (for the client). Sometimes that is in your best interest and sometimes it's not."

But the second reason got its start with Jack McGowan, a media representative for a trade magazine "C.E.E." I was assigned the Ideal Industries account in

Sycamore, Illinois, a long-time account for Sperry Boom, but I knew nothing about wire nuts, Yellow 77, etc. Jack said, "How would you like to learn about the industry and the role electrical distributors play but, more importantly, the companies that compete with Ideal?" **See Lesson 13 – Hold Your Clients Close but Hold Competitors Closer.** It turns out the CEO, Dennis and I were summoned to a meeting by the CEO and VP of Sales for Ideal Industries. Not a good sign! We thought we were going to be fired, but we kept the business because of the visits I had made with Jack McGowan. His son and I remained friends long after his passing. **See Lesson 14 – The Good, The Bad, and The Ugly.**

Family vacations were an important part of my early life as a kid. Each year we would go away somewhere for two weeks. One year we went to California to visit my dad's sister and her family. While there, we went to Disneyland and Knotts Berry Farm. But the vacations I remember most fondly are trips to northwest Wisconsin to stay at a resort called Brown's Cottages. Our family spent all our time fishing and socializing with our fellow resort guests the last two weeks in July until I went off to college. As a result, I always dreamed of owning a cottage somewhere on a lake when I got older.

In 1973 when Gerrie and I were still living in an apartment in Chicago, we received a cassette tape from my father. Since he had a lot to say, back in the day, sending a cassette tape was less expensive than a long-distance phone call. He told us about an old house that was for sale on Lake Chetac where we had always vacationed. He was willing to loan us the money to buy it. Gerrie thought both of us were insane! Eight hours by car to the lake from Chicago and we didn't even own a house? My dad's comment was, "God's making a lot of mini-bikes but he isn't making any more lakefront." So, we bought the house. **See Lesson 15 – Seize the Opportunity to Make Memories.**

Meanwhile the CEO at Sperry Boom hired a gentleman by the name of Barton Ladd from N.W. Ayer, a major agency in Chicago, as his heir apparent. He had run the U.S. Army account and was well-liked by everyone in the agency. He pushed all of us to get to the next level. Sperry Boom had moved downtown now, and I had an office at 625 N. Michigan Avenue. I was now making over $30,000 a year and had a wife and two daughters in the suburbs plus a cottage in Wisconsin.

As in many business situations, our CEO couldn't let go and turn things over to Bart. We all could feel how frustrated Bart was. He ended up leaving and went back to N.W. Ayer. He suggested I meet with another agency executive who worked for D'Arcy, MacManus & Masius (now part of Leo Burnett) by the name of Dick Stack. He was a management supervisor on Amoco Plastics looking for another account person. (Remember in the movie "The Graduate" when Mr. McGuire tells Ben he has just one word—"Plastics"?)

6

D'Arcy MacManus & Masius
Chicago and Minneapolis

I interviewed at D'arcy, McManus & Masius with Dick Stack and his boss Wally Ruckle, as well as David Keil, who was responsible for all of the Standard Oil Business. I liked all three of them and couldn't imagine working on a major brand like Amoco. I accepted their offer and started in 1974 with my own office on the 71st floor of the Standard Oil building at 200 E. Randolph (now the Aon Center). This office had a commanding view of Lake Michigan—a far cry from my tiny "closet/office/cubicle" at Sperry Boom! It was there that I would eventually meet Ed McMahon and Ted Turner.

    I encountered Ed McMahon in the Men's Room at the D'Arcy offices. What a great personality! Ted Turner, on the other hand, was crude and arrogant. He embarrassed me when I asked him a question during a meeting about getting approval for our ads on the network he was forming—CNN. His answer, laced with crass expletives and imagery, caused many of us to blush, especially the ladies in the room.

We now had a home in Arlington Heights and our daughter was going to preschool. Ron Boe and his wife Gina lived nearby so we were beginning to develop a circle of friends who all shared the same sorts of problems and challenges that young families face. Patrick and Mary Ann Dutcher (from my Army days) lived in nearby Waukegan, Illinois. They were our daughter's godparents so we got together frequently. We decided that Gerrie could stop working at Pfizer and stay home with Julie and soon-to-be-born Karen. I was now making enough money so that we could live on my salary.

I would take the train every day to the office, and things were going very well there and at home. Dick was a great teacher like Dennis, and I learned how to write and deliver presentations about "plastics." Our client, Joe Hanlon, was great. We would take him to lunch, and he would always come back after one of our lunches and whip out a can of Scotch Guard and spray his tie. He said this way his ties would never have to go to the cleaners.

Remember—I didn't write the ads, I didn't do the media plans, I didn't do the television commercials. I was referred to by the creative department as "The Bringer." My parents never understood what I did. My dad always thought it was "a pretend job," but he thought we must be doing OK because we were living in a nice house and we seemed to be doing fine.

I remember one day being summoned to the president's (Mr. Schubert's) office. He and Dave Keil asked me if I would like to be account supervisor on the Amoco Corporate account. No more plastics, just making TV ads telling the world how Amoco was looking for more oil all over the U.S., as we were right in the middle of the energy crisis, and everyone hated the oil companies. During my brief tenure (less than two years), every account supervisor on Amoco Corporate had either quit or been fired—three that I can recall! So I said, "Why not!" I was given a raise, and now I had no one like Dick and Dennis to protect me. Dave was there for moral support and helped me write my creative briefs, but it was up to me to "sell the creative" to the senior executives at Amoco. They were all in their 50's and 60's, and I was 30. Talk about a mismatch!

For my first meeting with Alan Groh, head of Amoco Public Affairs, I had three storyboards. These are drawings rendered by the art directors consisting of written dialogue below each picture explaining the narrative of the ad. I was given the rationale for each commercial by the creative department, and off I went to present them for approval to Mr. Groh. Production costs for each ad were around $50,000. So how did the meetings go, you ask? Well, I presented all three storyboards with supporting rationale. Mr. Groh listened and when I was finished, walked up to the easel from which I was working. He proceeded to tear each storyboard in half and put it under my arm. He said to tell the creative department he didn't like any of them! I was scared, if not terrified, when I walked the 55 floors back up to our office. I didn't take the elevator because I didn't want anyone to see me with my torn storyboards. I figured I would be the fourth account supervisor to be fired, or maybe I should just go back to Cedar Rapids where I was born and work at Wilson's on the second shift.

That turned out to be the worst meeting I would ever have with him. Eventually we became friends, and for over three years, we played racquetball together and produced some great television commercials. We made several trips to New York City and Washington, DC together. He was another great client whom I respected and from whom I learned corporate advertising.

I recognized at some point that my formal education in business in 1975 was severely lacking. I couldn't tell a balance sheet from a grocery list. D'Arcy offered to send me back to school for 2 years, full-time with salary. Bill Raidt, who was vice chairman, was behind this 100%. But I said "No, I'll go at night and get my MBA in Finance." since I already knew everything about marketing. **See Lesson 16 – Night School Resumes Belong on the Top of the Pile.**

I was quickly made aware of the fact and the reality that there were several management supervisors who were great at obtaining new clients for the agency. They were always on the prowl for new business. Today they're known as business development managers. Most of them talked a good story and made all kinds of claims about what they could do, but in reality, in my 40 years in the business, I have only known one or two who could even get an appointment, let alone a meeting and it usually involved alcohol! But these new business folks were special, always traveling and helping develop the pitch for the prospective client. So, I thought this is something I should try...because billing/revenue is power! How did I start? Every morning when I walked to the train, I passed the Weber Grill headquarters. I'll start there.

When I finally got a meeting with the Weber marketing director, Mike Kempster (he later became CEO), he said he was perfectly happy with their current agency. He did advise me to keep in touch, so I would drop in every month or so. Coffee, chit-chat, but no business...until one day when I stopped, he said, "Does your agency do market research? Do you do focus groups?" I went back to the office to talk with the research director, who immediately claimed the project as "<u>his</u> find." Wally Ruckle insisted I stay involved, so now everyone in the agency was my "friend." And some people made fun of me saying, "Let's get Dean a house near United Airlines!"

The research helped them build and modify their first gas kettle grill, which was a disaster but later turned into the Genesis product, which we have at our cottage. Weber was a great company with great people but no advertising—just a research project that the department touted as "new product development expertise" and gave them a good case history for new business presentations. I always made sure that in any of our case histories, we told the truth. The Weber gas grill story is a classic! Great research, no revenue stream, just a project, but I put it down as a success. If anything, it was a great boost to my self-esteem and helped me start thinking, "Maybe I can make it in this business!"

"Big Box" retailers were just getting started in 1974-75—K-Mart being the biggest, and a major customer for Weber. However, K-Mart would not allow Weber to increase the prices for the coming year. I was summoned to a meeting at Weber regarding how we could take costs out of manufacturing their Charcoal Kettle Cooker. I wasn't sure why I was there. I knew next to nothing about manufacturing costs. But I went and listened to engineers talk about cutting costs. I finally suggested, "What if we cut 1 to 2 inches off each one of the three stainless steel legs?" Everyone thought it was a great idea—but we couldn't do that every year!

I didn't realize it at the time, but I was witnessing the beginning of "price point retailing," which accounts for the cheapening of many products we buy today. In other words, "they don't make things like they used to." Weber, on the other hand, continues to make great products. After 70+ years, I am on my fourth Weber grill and Genesis II.

After four years of night school, I was just about to finish my MBA. I had only to re-take statistics because I dropped it when I was failing. Mr. Raidt came to my office and said, "Bloomfield Hills (near Detroit) is looking for someone to work in their accounting department, and now that you've got your MBA, we think you would be a good fit." I was shocked! I wanted to be a management supervisor, not an accountant! I said I would discuss it with my wife and he said, "OK, think about it." I went home that night and discussed it with Gerrie, and her reaction was, "No way are we moving to Detroit! We don't know anyone there! Besides, I thought you wanted to go to Minneapolis to be closer to the cottage. Why did we buy that place again?" We both had an emotional evening and agreed family came first. My chances of becoming a general manager in Chicago in an office that large were between "zero and none." Fortunately, D'Arcy had an office in Bloomington, Minnesota, and it was very small as Campbell Mithun, Carmichael Lynch, Bozell & Jacobs and Martin Williams dominated the market. Everyone in the agency business thought I was nuts—in fact, Alan Groh, my Amoco client, said, "Who did you piss off? I thought your career was doing great!" And it was. Family won out and trumped my career. **See Lesson 17 – Career Choices...Never Act Alone**.

But then it happened—Bill Rosenthal was going to be made head of the D'Arcy Minneapolis office. He was a management supervisor who was as "slick as they come." He was married to a drop-dead gorgeous lady who was the New York Times media representative for the Midwest. They were the quintessential power couple. He said, "Come to the Twin Cities. You'll be fine. We're building a great office there. I'm pulling together people from Chicago, and we're going to shake that town up." So, I started commuting back and forth from Arlington Heights to Bloomington, Minnesota. Our house sold right away. Gerrie came for a visit, and we looked at houses. We saw seven or eight, but the last one was one we could afford—an upgrade from our old house with attached double garage, basement and a grade school two blocks away. We made an offer and bought it, so now it was moving time.

We had just moved into our new house in suburban Minneapolis, when I had the opportunity to meet our new neighbors, Bill and Julie Bounds. Bill was an Army veteran and former Green Beret. We connected immediately as we were the only two veterans in our neighborhood. Bill could fix anything from a small pump on a fish tank to installing central air conditioning in the house we had just bought. Even though we have both moved years ago, Bill and Julie are still on my train today. I've learned a ton from Bill over the years, and he still jokingly calls me "Sir" as he was an enlisted man in the Army.

In the meantime, D'Arcy Minneapolis had landed the American Hoist & Derrick account. They made cranes and recycling equipment. (Remember the movie Goldfinger where the car gets crushed? That was an Amhoist/Harris press and shear!) Before we closed on the house, I flew Gerrie and the girls to Minneapolis for the weekend. We had a great dinner at Red Lobster and I went back to the apartment in which I had been staying. I opened the door and the phone was ringing. I answered it, and it was Bill Rosenthal, saying, "I'm headed to <u>New York City</u> tomorrow. I'm going to be head of the DM&M New York office. You'll be reporting to the new manager, Jim Vance."

I was in shock! I'd never met Jim, and all I knew was he was from Leo Burnett and ran the Kentucky Fried Chicken account. "Great," I thought, "I'm a business-to-business guy—cranes and chicken. At least they both begin with a "C!" I worked with another account supervisor, Mike Leonhardt, who was also from Chicago (the Marstellar Agency) but we were definitely "out-of-towners." I hired my first account executives—one of which I fired shortly thereafter and another who went on to have major jobs with McDonalds in the U.S. and Australia. But I was now a manager and had another account executive whom Jim wanted me to fire. I didn't. But I think my relationship with Jim was never the same after that, in spite of my serving our clients like Don Waack, who was a great guy. Jim always thought I was "too close" to the client.

DM&M Minneapolis at the time was full of characters—a research director who had forgotten more about market research than I would ever know, and several young people who later went on to be rock stars at other agencies in the Twin Cities.

Meanwhile, back at our house on Arbour Avenue, things were going pretty well. We had friends at church and, most importantly, our two daughters were doing great in school. My clients were great, but my boss, not so much. I always felt he looked down on me—my being from Iowa and his graduating from Notre Dame. On the other hand, he forced me to be a better account supervisor and brought discipline to the office to which we had never before been exposed—creative review boards, account reviews. These were things I would later implement at the offices and companies for which I would be responsible.

However, I was still an outsider in the ad community in the Twin Cities. That was until Steve Bergerson came into my office. He was recruiting for the local professional advertising organization, the Advertising Federation of Minnesota. The Ad Fed had over 600 members at the time from client companies, media companies, printing companies and other agencies! **See Lesson 18 - Leave Your Zip Code and Volunteer!**

Through Steve and the Ad Fed, I met Norma Cox, who had her own agency and was also an Ad Fed member. She connected me with a committee that ran a business-to-business forum with business publishers from all over the U.S., which was a major money maker for the Ad Fed. I got involved in meeting some great people in the business, including clients and numerous media representatives. At this event, Norma Cox introduced me to even more people in the Twin Cities. Ultimately, I became president of the Ad Fed, and was heavily involved in an advertising services tax bill with the state legislature, meeting several state senators and representatives. My most memorable meeting, however, was with the Speaker of the Senate, Doug Johnson, a DFL'er, who at our one and only meeting said he was most proud of the fact that he never "took a paycheck from the private sector!" Luckily, I never had the opportunity in my entire career to work with or for politicians. We did defeat the ad tax in committee by having all the local newspaper and radio stations testify regarding the impact it would have on their businesses. We had one or two businesses testify from the district of each senator on the committee. The bill died in committee. My take-away: "All business and politics is local." Don't ever forget that! Prior to the hearing on the bill, I did not incur a lot of favor with the egos of the large agencies or media companies, but my strategy had worked.

Things were going along OK at D'Arcy. We weren't getting any new business in spite of our best efforts. Then I got a call out of the blue from Ron Anderson, the creative director at Bozell & Jacobs in Minneapolis. He was the "Dean of the Creative Community" in the upper Midwest and wanted to have breakfast with me. We did…and I received a job offer right at breakfast.

7

Bozell and Kamstra

I came home and told my wife and daughters I was now moving on to a new agency, Bozell & Jacobs, and would be responsible for their business-to-business advertising and part of their new business team. I was no longer viewed as an "out-of-towner." I was finally accepted as a "local." I was thrilled. The head of the office, Paul Nelson, and I got along very well and stayed friends to this day. I could have worked for him for the rest of my career. By the way, I was now in my 30's, and the usual retirement age of an advertising executive was 45. I was still interacting with media representatives, and one day Tom Whelan with the Minneapolis Star Tribune said he wanted to meet me. He also was a transplant from Chicago, having worked for the Chicago Tribune. He knew many of the same people in Chicago I did. We became instant friends. After 42 years, he is still riding my train. In fact, he and his wife, Marty, are riding in the first car. The thing I remember about our first meeting was he wanted to "get involved in the community." Well, it turns out he got involved with the Advertising Federation of Minnesota and won their Silver Medal award. (There is no gold.) You'll hear more about him and his wife Marty in Chapter 16.

One day I was in the office when I was told David Bell was coming to visit from New York. David started his career in the Minneapolis office but now lived in New York where he was the Number 2 person at Bozell & Jacobs. Ron Anderson had left for New York as their creative director. I was sent to meet with hardware store executives about carrying Wagner paint spraying products as part of a new business pitch which they had dropped in the past. I was lucky enough to convince one buyer from St. Louis Central Hardware to do so. When David heard what I had done, he said, "You'll get the business!" We did, which began a 25-year client-agency relationship with Wagner Spray Tech, Carl Cooper and his wife, Pat. We are still friends to this day. That was in 1985. I didn't hear from David again until 1997 when he wrote me a 17-page letter. More on that later.

Another phone call I received in 1986 was from Ken Kamstra, who had a small business-to-business agency in St. Paul and Austin, Texas. He was starting to put together a succession plan for his company and wanted to meet me. Kamstra was a good agency with good people and a good creative product but had a very low profile. The meetings began with Ken and several of his executives, again all good people. But the people

I met with were all interested in continuing to do what they had been doing without calling too much attention to themselves or their clients. Ken didn't feel that way. He wanted to change that, so all of a sudden, I was made the executive vice president in 1986 and ultimately president, responsible for both offices.

I honestly felt I had trained all my life for this job/company, plus I bought in and was a stockholder, meaning my name was "on the line" with the bank. There was one problem. We were not growing, and things were about to get worse. Agencies' client budgets are completely dependent upon the success of those businesses. As one client remarked, "The company factory in Ft. Wayne needs a new roof. Guess where the money will come from—the ad budget!" That budget was totally disappearing. In 1988 prospects for Kamstra were not looking good until a media representative suggested I contact John Cashmore with the Weyerhauser Corporation. He was having problems with his current agency. **See Lesson 19 – You Ain't Learnin' Nothin' when You're Talkin'.**

The good news was the staff we had was excellent. In fact, we had recruited two of the best creative talents in the Twin Cities—an art director, Bob Kay, and the best writer I have ever worked with in my entire career, Dan Haag. (His wife Missie would later be my administrative assistant.) For that reason, I was feeling very confident about soliciting new accounts and was ready to meet John Cashmore. So, the courtship began with several informal get-togethers (that involved alcohol) before he gave us the go-ahead on several projects. This blossomed into a 20-year relationship and, more importantly, a long-lasting friendship. John came to us at a time when we really needed the revenue--our darkest hour, so to say. He was tough, but fair, outspoken, but genuine, in his appreciation for the work we did. He, along with Roy Doering at Hurd Windows, are two of my all-time favorite clients.

Roy died in 2020 and John passed away in 2021. One of my favorite memories is traveling with Roy to Arnold Palmer's home in Latrobe, Pennsylvania in 1985 and seeing all the green jackets in his closet and the trophies! But off of his den was a door to a large closet with shelves full of every imaginable model airplane and helicopter, both civilian and military. There were 747's, Huey helicopters, etc. Mr. Palmer said this was the room he was most proud of. When I asked him why, he said, "Being a pilot, I've flown every one of these airplanes." I said, "Even an "F-4 phantom jet?" He replied, "Generals like to play golf too!"

Having John Cashmore's business was a real turning point for Kamstra. We started gaining accounts and adding employees. It was a terrific time for the company. We went from 15-20 employees to over 70, but with growth came issues and problems. I felt I needed to get some outside perspective on running a business. A friend, Jim Secord, recommended I hook up with an organization called TEC (The Executive Committee), which was specifically designed for small companies and entrepreneurs. Members would meet monthly and share their problems and issues with other presidents, CEO's and owners and ask for advice. Jack Sell was "the chair" of our group. He was a terrific businessman in his previous career and acted as our facilitator and coach. I learned a great deal from him. This group of business leaders (about 10 to 12 people) acted as my personal board of directors. **See Lesson 20 – Look Before You Leap.**

Regarding personnel, what a mine field that has become for most managers, starting with employee reviews, which lead to promotions and salary increases. Have I gotten your attention yet? As a manager, it was the most difficult and time-consuming activity in which I was involved. The written evaluation, the salary guidelines, different levels, 360 evaluations, bonus calculations and formulas—all based upon those magic words, "is this appropriate" or, my favorite, "fair?" And to the recipient of the review, "it was never enough!" (Always unspoken.)

My father suffered a stroke in 1993 and was paralyzed on his left side. He had been extremely active until this point. He was 90 years old. All of a sudden, I became aware of my own mortality! For the next two years, my wife and I made trips back and forth to visit my mother and father. My sister was living not too far away and handled everything—meals, bills, paperwork—as my dad went in and out of the nursing home. He would get a little better, and we would bring him home, and then he would regress and we would have to take him back. He died in 1995 at the age of 92.

I must confess that up until this point in my life and my career, I really never understood employees or people who dealt with ailing parents! Frequently I was not very sympathetic or understanding, but eventually that all changed for me! Until you've been through this kind of situation yourself, you don't have any empathy for people who go through these hardships. I had any number of people experience this kind of thing in my career, and I can say I never again was critical of them. My wife experienced some serious health issues several years later, and, luckily, my bosses, David Bell and Gene Bartley, supported me when I was "absent from duty" for several months. Times have changed to some extent today with medical leaves, etc. for any number of companies and organizations, but in those days it was rare.

At Kamstra, one of our managers suggested I meet Dr. Bruce Roselle, a trained psychologist, who could assist us in understanding and improving employee performance. Mr. Kamstra had set up a very orderly transition in ownership to four of us over a period of seven years. It was a good plan; however, as we grew, it became apparent that if we were to continue to grow, we needed to broaden the ownership to ensure that we didn't lose any of those key individuals.

Our writer and assistant creative director, Dan Haag, was the first to leave, and I was convinced this was only the beginning of the exodus. My TEC group chair and the other members of my group suggested that we bring in an outside accountant (Mr. Kamstra's brother-in-law was our CFO) and do an audit to determine the status of the agreement and the payment as we continued to have record-breaking years and growth. The other shareholders did not agree with me or see the need for an outside review. I decided to leave Kamstra, but I knew it would take a while to find something else.

The experience I obtained at Kamstra from 1985 until I departed in 1996 was invaluable to me as a manager. I could have never been more prepared for what lay ahead of me had I not had the experience as the president of Kamstra. Ken clearly was my stepping stone to the next level of my development. **See Lesson 21 – A Word About Agreements & Founders of Successful Companies.**

8

Gage

Later in the spring of 1996, I received a call from a search firm that Gage Marketing was interested in finding a general manager to run their advertising and sales promotion division. I knew very little about sales promotion, but Gage was a great company. I applied and after two meetings with Tom Belle and Skip Gage, I was hired with a letter of agreement and a bonus structure that was better than what I had at Kamstra. It involved no ownership, but had a great bonus plan and plenty of incentives if I could grow the business like we had done at Kamstra. Now all I had to do was meet the employees and get started.

I asked Tom and Skip Gage if I could bring in Dr. Roselle and have him do an assessment of my key managers. I also asked if I could use Dan Haag as our creative director. They agreed to both. Dan was an immediate hit, and Bruce did his interviews and assessments. I anxiously awaited the results. I had been there about six months and had just received my starting bonus, but hadn't cashed the check. It was substantial, but I was interested in getting Bruce's reports on the individuals with whom he met and his assessments of how I was doing in their eyes. I couldn't wait for that meeting with Bruce. I knew I could always improve as a manager, but I had started to run the department like an agency and put in place a number of disciplines and processes. I was anxious to get some feedback. Skip and Tom had been complimenting me, and at the company Christmas party at our townhouse, everyone came and had a great time!

Surprisingly, at this point my train went off the rails. Bruce started our meeting off by saying, "No one wants you at Gage. They don't like you or any of the changes you are making. Skip and Tom might like you but the others don't. You have no opportunity for success there based on what the people told me!"

Meanwhile, things were not going well at Kamstra, and at Bozell Minneapolis. Both offices were losing business. David Bell and the CFO of Bozell Minneapolis met with Mr. Kamstra and the remaining shareholders. They discussed selling the operation to True North, a holding company, like D'Arcy did when they sold their Bloomington office to Bozell.

Following the meeting, the CFO of Bozell Minneapolis reached out to me and asked if I would be interested in running a combined operation of Bozell and Kamstra. I said I would be more than happy to consider their proposal. David Bell then wrote me a 17-page letter outlining what he envisioned for this new company. It would be named Bozell Kamstra and ultimately would consist of several offices in the U.S. and eventually outside the U.S.! The CFO immediately offered me the presidency of this new brand with a signing bonus if I accepted. I accepted.

The next day, I met with Skip and Tom and returned their bonus check. It hurt, but ethically it was the right thing to do. This entire sequence of events—receiving the Gage bonus, Bruce's report, David's letter and subsequent offer, and my acceptance—happened in 10 business days! So, I was about to leave one car on the train and get into another one, one that would impact me for the remainder of my business career.

9

Bozell Kamstra

It was 1997 and I was back at Bozell. Many of the same people I knew before were still there and welcomed me back. The same goes for the remaining people at Kamstra, many of whom I had hired before. So for me, it was like a dream come true. I still remember driving back from Iowa in a new convertible I had bought for Gerrie. (We had been doing business with this car dealership since 1988 and still do today!) I was thinking I finally have a position I have trained for all my life.

I was able to re-connect with all my former clients (3M, Hurd Windows), and the people in the Austin, Texas office (Kerry Hilton and Mike McCullar, who along with Jack Stanton ran our public relations activities), plus all the Bozell clients (Wagner Spray Tech, Elkay Cabinets) and a new client, Schwann Foods! I met Andrew Deal, probably the best marketing strategist I have ever known. (More about him later.) To this day, he, Mike and Jack have been my friends, and we still talk from time to time.

David Bell and Gene Bartley proceeded to give me more responsibilities and more offices to oversee (Dallas, Pittsburgh, Cleveland, Boston) and a presence in New York City. At the same time when this was going on, David was made CEO of True North, and I was to report to a man in New York by the name of Gene Bartley. I ended up working for him for the next 12 years. But first let me talk about our initial meeting. It was in his New York City office at Bozell where he now had responsibility for all the Bozell offices in the U.S. including Bozell Kamstra. His reputation preceded him as someone you didn't want to get on the "wrong side" of. He had no time for excuses or fools. And as David said, he was the best judge of "horse flesh" (meaning people) he ever knew!

This first meeting was very informal. Gene asked me about my background, and I briefly recounted my move from Chicago to Minneapolis with DM&M. He replied that he had previously worked for DM&M. I told him that my memories of DM&M were not very good. I told him my story about Bill Rosenthal luring me to Minneapolis, etc. and shortly thereafter calling me and basically saying, "Good luck!" and then leaving for another job. Gene then looked at me and said, "I fired Bill Rosenthal!" After the meeting, I immediately called Gerrie and said, "I think this new boss is going to work out just fine!"

Gene clearly was the best boss I ever had. He would be the first to chew me out if I had done something wrong (never in front of other people, however) and the first to praise me if I had done something right. The lessons I learned in those twelve years could fill up a college textbook. Some of my favorites: We were involved in retaining a piece of business. The client requested that we reduce our rates but keep the same level of service. Gene said, "Sorry, we don't need the practice!" This is a line I have passed onto people in our business and especially service providers like plumbers, electricians, contractors, etc. who constantly are pressed to reduce their prices.

Another classic line from Gene has to do with managers and dealing with problems they face. In many cases, that manager thinks he or she can solve the problem given more time and attention without requesting help or assistance. What happens? The problem only gets worse and then oftentimes there is nothing anyone can do to solve it. Gene's line was always, "Go ugly, go early!" <u>Never</u> surprise your boss with a problem. Then he or she respects you and you'll be fine.

Also, the most important thing you have to have in any relationship, starting at home with your family and kids, is trust. Gene and I still have that relationship 25 years later. We had just landed a major piece of business in Minneapolis, and there was a group of people who wanted to take it to New York. They requested a meeting with Gene and David without my being present and told them I was not telling the truth about what was going on. The meeting was over before it started. David said to them, "In the 20 years I have known Dean Buresh, he has never lied to me."

Trust—the most important component in any relationship.

Our older daughter had graduated from the University of Iowa and had obtained a Master's degree in information science at Illinois. She got married and was working in New York for Find/SVP, a market research firm. Our younger daughter was graduating from high school and was applying to colleges for admission. **See Lesson 22 – What's Next after High School?**

When the new brand Bozell Kamstra was formed, it included officers of successful companies who had been independent businessmen and women. So, the first thing we agreed upon besides coming together was the need for building a new culture. Because I was constantly traveling to the various offices pitching new business, my schedule was very complicated. I needed to make travel arrangements and handle a ton of correspondence and requests for information. I was lucky enough to convince Missie Haag (the wife of Dan Haag) to be my administrative assistant. She clearly made my life much easier, keeping track of all the details and, most importantly, a ton of confidential information that I was now responsible for. She also made sure that the people I needed to see and meet with were taken care of. She was a huge asset for me and the organization. I also was able to convince the media director in Omaha, David Dasenbrock, to come to Minneapolis and become our overall media director for all the offices. He is still on my train today. One of his greatest strengths was his ability to mentor and develop his staff. He was one of the best managers I ever had in any capacity.

When interactive businesses were just getting started, and we were fortunate enough to have Suburu and the U.S. Air Force as our interactive clients, I was convinced that this new medium was going to change everything. We would be going forward as an agency and as a business. Interactive marketing combines the internet with cell phones, and we were on the edge of a new beginning of customers taking control of the relationship with marketers. The rules had just changed; customers now had the power. I was to learn shortly that the power that brands had enjoyed was also about to change.

I was also spending more time in New York as David had suggested I become a board member for the B.P.A. (Business Publishers Association). The B.P.A. was a non-profit association of business and consumer publications that audited the circulation of print publications and websites. Glen Hanson was the CEO, and his board consisted of publishers, client companies and advertising agencies. This was my first board position, and did I learn a lot! Glenn taught me how to structure and run a successful board meeting. I also learned the importance of rehearsing for meetings with staff and anticipating questions from the board members. Ultimately, I became chairman of the board—one of, if not the, most professional boards on which I had the honor to serve. Glenn and I still maintain contact, and he is still on my train today.

I happened to be in New York one day with our older daughter Julie. We were riding the subway back to her apartment in Brooklyn. A woman got on the car that we were in. She knew Julie from Find/SVP and was now employed at Ernst & Young. She suggested Julie should come to EY for an interview because they were looking for analysts just like Julie. Eighteen years later Julie is an associate director there. I guess it was fate, like my friend Dennis having a drink with Gerrie and completely changing the course of my whole life.

It was 1999, and things were rolling along nicely in spite of all the cultural issues we had faced. We had continued to grow at a rate of 30%. How could things get any better?

10

Fujitsu

His name was Wayne Moles, from Nebraska. It was 1988. He unexpectedly came into my life in Minneapolis from California, recommended by Kathryn Lewis, who ran the Bozell office in Santa Clara, California. He was employed by a Japanese agency called Asian Advertisers and was re-locating to the Twin Cities. He wondered if we would be interested in partnering with his firm on the Fujitsu account globally. Wayne thought Fujitsu would be looking for a global partner in the near future for a global corporate advertising campaign. He moved into our office space in Butler Square, and so the pursuit of a global account began. I had virtually no global experience, and Ron Anderson, the creative director, had very little. But with Gene and David's support, we were "all in." Soon the monthly trips to Tokyo began for Wayne and me to meet the prospective client and our partners, Asian Ads!

Looking back, I think everyone in New York thought we were crazy even attempting to pitch this business. When we won it ($500 million over four to five years), everyone was in shock. Global broadcast and print, commercials shot in Brazil, Olympic sponsorship for the 2000 games, Fujitsu jazz festivals, dinners in Japanese homes, karaoke in Japanese bars (I couldn't sing but I would imitate Louie Armstrong singing "What a Wonderful World"), cobras in the lawn at a client's home in Singapore, one Japanese wedding, one Japanese funeral, and Ijun-san wondering if we have a lot of prostitutes in Minnesota because he saw women smoking outdoors (Only prostitutes do that in Japan)—just some of the adventures during that period of time.

As the Fujitsu account grew, we needed to hire a full-time creative director in New York. Wayne identified an individual who he thought was appropriate because he was liked by the Japanese client. I informed Gene of my decision to hire that person upon which he replied, "I'd like to meet him!" I responded, "You don't trust my judgment?" "No!" he said, "I just want to meet him so I can defend his salary to the Board as I have never hired someone who is making more money than you!" Gene was just trying to protect me, but I was too ignorant at the time to figure that out. It's always good to have the boss in the boat with you when you're making a major hire, especially when that person will be making more than you!

We continued to need more account service support in New York as we now had retained Ted Bates, another agency, to handle our international work since FCB (Foote Cone & Belding) had Compaq as their client, which presented a conflict. After sampling a number of New York management supervisors, we went outside the firm and hired Niland Mortimer, who had a ton of global experience. He made a great partner for Wayne since he was now on the Bozell Kamstra payroll. I could now rest easier knowing that we had a creative director in New York and now another management supervisor. Then my whole world was turned upside down!

11

Bozell/New York

Interpublic bought True North after the Chrysler business went to BBD&O, part of Omnicom. Needless to say, that changed everything. Interpublic also had numerous brands from all the acquisitions they had made, so offices and companies and cities were being consolidated at a rapid rate.

In the last True North annual report, Bozell Kamstra went from the inside front cover with a 30% annual growth rate and $250 million in billings to oblivion. Our offices all over the U.S. were consolidated into other Interpublic companies. For example, Bozell Kamstra Minneapolis became part of Carmichael Lynch and Bozell Kamstra Dallas became part of Temerlin McClain, etc. Unfortunately, some outstanding people were let go. It was probably the most difficult situation I had ever encountered in my entire career. We had been so successful at building a brand, Bozell

Kamstra, in such a short period of time. Needless to say, in every city in which we had a presence, companies and offices wanted our clients and some of our key players. But most importantly, they wanted our revenue because in almost every city and every office, our margins were great.

Temerlin McLain was not interested in the Austin office—only the Dallas office and in Sixty Foot Spider, an interactive agency. The folks in Austin, led by Kerry Hilton, were cut loose with their client list, so they formed their own agency. More on that later.

Meanwhile, Bozell New York wanted Fujitsu, so Wayne Moles, our CFO, and I packed our bags and headed to New York. Niland and Glenn were already there, so it was a move that made good business sense. But to say goodbye to Bob Kay, David Dasenbrock, Jack Stanton, Katherine Johnson, Mike McCullar, and Missie Haag wasn't easy. To this day, it was a very difficult thing to do. How do you explain to everyone that we did everything right and still got dissolved?

12

New York

I had never thought I would be moving to New York. Frankly I had tried to avoid it my entire career. I guess I was intimidated by the city, the level of talent that existed there, and afraid that I would fall short and end my career in disgrace. So, I rented an apartment on the Upper West Side near Lincoln Center, and my office was on 23rd Street (now a Home Depot). I took the subway to the office every day when I wasn't traveling for Fujitsu. Incidentally, the movie "Big" was filmed in our office. I had a new administrative assistant, Jackie Alexander, originally from Trinidad who was a former police officer there. She was perfect like Missie. She got to know me and our clients. She was well-liked by everyone and stayed with me until I left Interpublic in 2008. More on that later.

Gene now left Bozell per his contract when there was a change in ownership of True North so I now reported to Tom Bernardin, president of Bozell New York. He later went on to become CEO of Leo Burnett. Niland and Wayne were especially busy with Fujitsu, but we did manage to get Novartis Animal Health in North Carolina as a client because of a prior relationship I had in Minneapolis. "Celebrex for dogs" was our product and we did very well.

But another change was coming. Tom departed for Leo Burnett and Gene returned as Foote Cone & Belding's executive in charge of all their U.S. offices as well as their sales promotion companies. Bozell New York lost the Bank of America account, and they were going to close Bozell New York! What about Fujitsu? Well, it was off to Foote Cone & Belding with Jackie, Wayne and Niland. How Wayne and Niland were able to manage all those changes with the Japanese, I will never know. It speaks to the strength of the relationship they had built. The relationship with Fujitsu ended in 2007.

Wayne departed for the client side and now resides in Jacksonville, Florida, the chief story-teller for B Line.com, a transport logistics company. Niland became a management supervisor at FCB on Hewlett Packard and left there in 2015. He has become the director of marketing and communications at Fletcher School of Law and Diplomacy at Tufts in Boston. He also teaches a number of courses on digital and neurological marketing. These two individuals, along with Andy Deal from Schwann Foods, are three of the best marketing strategists I have ever known. They are still on my train after 23 years. We talk regularly. Visit them on LinkedIn. They are amazing!

13

Marketing Drive

Because FC&B had Compaq as a computer client, Fujitsu was "parked" under the Marketing Drive umbrella to prevent a conflict of interest. Client conflicts ruled the day.

Gene remembered that I had sales promotion and internet experience with Gage and Sixty Foot Spider and convinced the president of FCB, Brendon Ryan, that I should be made president of Marketing Drive Worldwide. They were having a number of issues with several of the offices in the U.S., and they wanted me to pull the organization together. Unlike Bozell Kamstra, where I had profit and loss responsibilities for all the offices in the Marketing Drive organization, I had P & L for some offices and for others, a "dotted line." **See Lesson 23 – Beware of the Dotted Line.**

Unlike Bozell Kamstra, none of the Marketing Drive offices wanted to work together, and all of them were solely concerned with their own P & L's and that of the local FCB office. Combine this with the fact that sales promotions were starting to take more and more dollars away from brand advertising budgets and, especially, for consumer package goods products. So, the advertising people in the agencies treated us like "lepers," even though we lived in the same village. At the same time, the fun was just starting with the major retailers because they had now become brands all unto themselves. More importantly, they had direct access to the consumer through their outlets and locations. All of a sudden, the words "private label" struck fear into the hearts of brand managers, the shining knights of the branding world.

Yes, I sat in many a meeting with "the buyer" from a major retailer where those words are muttered from the buyer to the brand or product manager, "In a perfect world, I wouldn't give you a price increase!" A word about "private labels"—**See Lesson 24 – Private Labels…Not So Bad.** Some marketers like Wagner Spray Tech continued to invest in branding and television advertising, but most began to make the gradual shift to interactive media and sales promotion.

Marketing Drive did give me the opportunity to continue to expand my global experience in the Far East, namely Hong Kong, and some outstanding consumer product accounts like Nautilus Exercise Equipment. I also got to grow my relationship with Wagner Spray Tech. Interpublic was involved in another re-alignment, David had left, Gene was getting ready to leave, Fujitsu had left, and I had made numerous changes in the offices I had P & L responsibility for.

I had put a succession plan in place for the organization, and I knew it was time to leave. So I departed and moved from New York to Chicago to focus more on the Midwest, but once again, it was extremely difficult to make any changes—no responsibility. As the CFO of FCB, Ed Harrigan, and I put together the forecast for Marketing Drive for 2008, he said, "Do you realize you will account for 15 to 20% of FCB's profit on revenue of less than $50 million?" Interpublic needed cash, so Marketing Drive was sold as I was going out the door.

The changes I saw coming were nothing compared to what has happened since 2008-2009. Two books worth reading are written by Ken Auletta. One is titled *Googled: The End of the World as We Know It.* His other management book is *Frenemies*. In these two books, he writes not only about the people in our business but all the changes in how advertising and sales promotion have changed and shifted dramatically—i.e., the consumer now has control and how we have gone from "Mad Men" to "Math Men!" As a consumer, be sure to read page 303 of the *Frenemies* book!

14

The World of Private Equity

I had walked out the door of Interpublic on a high note. Several of my executives had ended up in great organizations like Google and Facebook and onto a board of a privately held company that was a digital asset management company. I was 62, and I had stayed long beyond the life expectancy of an advertising "suit." Ed Harrigan had encouraged me to write a business plan before departing Interpublic, and, specifically, what I wanted to do after I retired. So, I took a crack at it. In the business plan, I wasn't very specific other than I wanted to do some consulting work and non-profit work until I was 75. Writing a book was not even a passing thought.

Kerry Hilton in Austin had renamed the Austin Bozell Kamstra office to HCB Health and was focusing all of his efforts in the healthcare space. He started with a little over $1 million in revenue and asked me to be on his board of directors. I agreed. Kerry is still on my train 24 years later although I relinquished the board seat in 2018. I'd like to think my mentoring helped him as he developed from a young creative director into a talented and successful CEO. It was only recently in 2020 that Kerry published his first novel, *Brothers of the Island*, and now has published four more novels, all of which can be found on Amazon. *Brothers of the Island* is a fiction novel about growing up with his grandfather in La Crosse, Wisconsin. He has become an excellent writer. I have always looked at Kerry as my "second son!" Get a copy of *The Brothers of the Island* and read about the Buresh Bakery!

I hadn't been gone from Interpublic for 30 days when David Bell (now an Advertising Hall of Fame member) and a private equity firm reached out to me about putting together a business-to-business network of agencies as nothing like this had been done in that "space." I was convinced that this could be done because the holding companies were heavily focused on business-to-consumer products and services, which were sexier and more glamorous than selling to business. Because of my experiences, the search was on for candidates in the U.S. and abroad. David and I spent the next 12 to 18 months traveling all over the U.S. trying to persuade the owners of numerous agencies how, by forming a B2B network, we could then in turn "flip it" to one of the major holding companies. By doing this, their stock would be worth considerably more than if they continued to operate independently.

Rick Segal was the CEO of HSR in Cincinnati. He was

the person, along with his partners, to sign up for our "vision." Like Kerry, Rick is still on my train today. HSR was the "perfect" business-to-business agency with offices in Cincinnati and Chicago, serving clients all over the U.S. We should have focused on acquiring more business-to-business agencies. We certainly had plenty of opportunities nationally.

However, the clock was ticking with the private equity folks to make more acquisitions faster, as the principals wanted money invested quickly so they could start getting their returns faster. In hindsight, we made a couple of fundamental mistakes. First, when buying HSR, we did extensive due diligence, meeting and interviewing their clients. The next two acquisitions we did <u>not</u> do a good job of due diligence. In fact, with one of the acquisitions, we did no client interviews. We didn't have any idea about how they were perceived or valued by the agency, not even one client/agency benchmark. And this would turn out to be the largest acquisition we made with the private equity firm!

I was the CEO of this group of companies, but in name and title only. After two years, I was asked to leave as I was not adding any value and was perceived by the companies we purchased as a problem and a hindrance to their overall growth. In other words, I was just "expensive overhead." **See Lesson 25– Are You Being Fitted for Roller Skates?**

The good news part of my exit package was an arrangement that when I referred any business to the companies, I would receive a commission because of previous relationships with numerous agencies and clients. I was able to have a very comfortable revenue stream for the next two years.

How did it turn out? What's the outcome? Everyone at the private equity firm was fired, and the companies we bought were sold to a large agency holding company...but my train still has David and Rick on it.

15

Life After Private Equity

At this point, I was 67, started drawing Social Security and would become a "consultant"—a term I had always loathed. When I heard someone say they were a consultant, my stereotype of these people was, "OK, they had been fired!" Bingo, I was now one of them. They were too old or between jobs—i.e., unemployed and were looking for their next "full-time opportunity." No, you're either employed or retired. I remember in Chicago when one of the Standard Oil executives would go to any business gathering involving name tags, on his, he would write "unemployed" in small letters beneath his name. People stayed away from him as if he had leprosy!

After a few months, the phone started to ring and, frankly, I was surprised. Former clients and several agencies called and wanted me to consult with them.

I was thrilled! Besides, Gerrie was anxious to get me out of the house. But the best part was, for the first time in my career, I could pick and choose who I wanted to work for! I was beholden only to myself.

I've had just about every psychological test done on me in the military and civilian world. As Dr. Bruce Roselle would say, "Dean will tell you what he thinks. You may not agree, but you will always know where you stand." Another great line of his was, "When I ask you 'How are you?', it's not a form of a greeting. I really want to know how you are!" My advice: just be careful. People don't want to hear an "organ recital."

I've been involved in numerous consulting assignments since the private equity world, and in every one of the situations, I felt like I added value and have enjoyed the people. Besides continuing to work with Dan Haag, I have enjoyed working with Andrew Deal and, most recently, Will Prest of KWP Consulting. These three individuals are some of the best marketers I have ever known in my career. I cannot say enough good things about all three of them. One other person I had the opportunity to meet and enjoy working with is Jafar Azmayesh. He has become a very successful entrepreneur and financial analyst—a University of Iowa graduate who is always on the lookout for good business ideas and is a master at execution. And, yes, they're all still on my train! As is Patrick Venetucci, who worked at Leo Burnett and is now CEO of Merge. (Patrick happens to be the son-on-law of Dennis Faltis who got me started in advertising.)

Per my business plan, I wanted to stop my consulting work at age 75, and I was getting close now. I enjoyed my time on the board of HCB in Austin and Meta Communications in Iowa, thanks again to Gregg Hammann, another former client.

16

Giving Back

You've all heard the expressions "Pay it forward", "Get involved," or "Give back." I think these admonitions are more important now than ever before, given the overall state of our country and the world. The Covid-19 pandemic has only amplified for all of us the need to "get involved." I've often said, "Do you like bacon and eggs? The chicken is involved, but the pig is committed!" Be a pig! It's not so much about the amount of money you're able to give to a cause or organization. It's about your time, because that is the single-most important commodity you have to offer.

We have two very good friends, Tom and Marty Whelan, who volunteer and give their time in a number of ways—from working at a food shelf, packing and moving the belongings of people transitioning to assisted living, mashing 600 pounds of Thanksgiving potatoes for Meals on Wheels, to driving people for appointments or errands. None of these are easy assignments. We need to thank people like them for what they do. Talk about giving back!

Ironically enough, my parents started volunteering in 1969 at Mercy Hospital in Cedar Rapids before my father retired. They worked evenings in the library researching for doctors, filing, copying and took a pause in 1975 when the library went to full-time staffing. They returned in 1976 to volunteer services doing everything from patient visits, bingo sessions and working in the gift shop. They volunteered until the 80's, officially re-retiring in 1990. My dad died in 1995 at age 92, and my mom passed in 2005.

There is an old saying, "The apple doesn't fall far from the tree." Following their example, my volunteering began at Methodist Hospital after my wife nearly died there from pneumonia in 2011. She was in intensive care for ten days but pulled through. I first became involved with the Foundation's hospital gown re-design project and now serve on the board.

Everyone talks about role models today with way too much emphasis and press devoted to professional athletics. The real role models should be the people who deliver healthcare services to our communities, our fire fighters, law enforcement personnel, and the truck drivers who deliver anything we want to our doors, just to name a few. Equally important are the teachers in our lives who come in all shapes and forms. These are people who mold us and help us grow.

We've all known some great people that we at one time called our friends, but, for whatever reason, never stayed connected. The pandemic gave me the time to re-connect with many of these special people and inspired me to write this book. Perhaps it gave you new reasons to be grateful—for good teachers and good people. I hope you've enjoyed my train ride as much as I have writing about it. I can honestly say I have truly "lived the dream!"

EPILOGUE

After you have read this book, I hope you will take the time to write down the teachers who have helped you achieve and attain the things in your life that you thought most meaningful. If these people are still alive, it surely wouldn't hurt to write them a note—not an e-mail or text—thanking them and explaining to them why you wrote them a note and the impact they had on you and your development as a person.

While writing this book during the Covid-19 pandemic, I lost one of my best friends, David Phillips. He was an Iowa farmer. I knew him through his sister, Mary Yoshioka, for over 20 years. We shared so many good times together visiting, fishing, and deer hunting in Iowa and Texas. He never once asked me much about what I did for a living. We just enjoyed being together. He always made me laugh. I wasn't ready for him to get off my train. Luckily, his wife Karen is still on it. I wish I would have had a chance to tell him how much he meant to me.

MUST READS

The Deepest Well by Nadine Burke Harris
Thanks! by Robert A. Emmons
Smoking Meats by Jeff Phillips
Frenemies by Ken Auletta
Googled: The End of the World as We Know It by Ken Auletta
The Hilarious World of Depression by John Moe
Brothers of the Island by Kerry Hilton

MY TEACHERS

Jackie Alexander
Ron Anderson
Jafar Azmayesh
Gene Bartley
Uncle Smokey
Becicka
David Bell
Tom Belle
Steve Bergerson
Clarence Bergman
Tom Bernardin
Fred Bertschinger
Ron & Gina Boe
Andy Boubin
Bill Bounds
Brett Boyum
Dr. Paul & Glennys
   Brimmer
Ed Briner
Mike Brugh
Bob Bruley
Andy Bubon
Steve Bures
Ernie Buresh
Gerrie Buresh
Joe Buresh
Julie Buresh
Lester Buresh
Charles Campbell
Carol Carbonneau
John Cashmore
John Conzemius
Prof. Archibald
   Coolidge
Carl Cooper
Norma Cox
Mike Cripe
Sgt. Bobby Dalrymple
David Dasenbrock
Andrew Deal
Mrs. Dee
Jeremy Dodge
Roy Doering
Pat Dutcher
Jack & Margo Edl
Prof. Donald Ehninger

Mrs. Evans
Pat Fallon
Dennis Faltis
Jim Felthouse
Jerry Franklin
Coach Roger
   Freeman
Skip Gage
Dan Gahlon
Glenn Hanson
Don & Elie Grant
Alan Groh
Dan & Missie Haag
Ken Halgren
Greg Hammann
Ed Harrigan
Kerry Hilton
Louis Hrdlicka
Don Jennings
Jim Jennings
Doug Johnson
Katherine Johnson
Ken Kamstra
David Kapvil
Bob Kay
David Keil
Mike Kempster
Karen Koch
Barton Ladd
Gary Langhurst
Bob Langridge
Coach Leigh
Steve Lendman
Mike Leonhardt
Katherine Lewis
Tom & Lynda Lynch
Jim Mallon
Ken Marsh
Mike McCullar
Jack McGowan
Wayne Moles
Niland Mortimer
Cpt. Ed Moses
Zach Myers
Paul Nelson
Ted Neuhouse

Bill & Mary Ann
   Niichel
Regina Niichel
Dick Parsons
David & Karen
   Phillips
Sgt. Pickup & family
Will Prest
Coach Purcell
Mrs. Rademacher
Bill Raidt
Ann Roberson
Bruce Roselle
Bill Rosenthal
Wally Ruckle
Brendon Ryan
Walter Schleuter
John Schubert
Jack Schutz
Lon Scriven
Jim Secord
Gene Seehusen
Rick & Adrien Segal
Jack Sell
Patrick Shirley
Harvey Smyth
Scott Spaeth
Dick Stack
Dave Stanek
Jack Stanton
Howard Strong
Dick Strubel
Monica Sullivan
Norm Van Broklin
Jim Vance
Patrick Venetucci
Don Waack
Ernesto & Berta
   Weaver
Bill Wendling
Tom & Marty Whelan
Sam Wiley
Max Willet
Jim Willis
Seiji & Mary Yoshioka
Ernie Zeisiger

WHAT I HAVE LEARNED

Lesson 1 – Invest with Your Head, Not Your Heart

Our first investments were savings bonds. I was in the Army, and all soldiers were required to buy one savings bond a month. The amount was automatically deducted from our paychecks. When I was discharged, I immediately cashed in those bonds as we needed money for the down payment on our first house. As everyone knows, in those early years, you live from paycheck to paycheck. Covering family expenses was a challenge, and it seemed like during the first five years of our marriage, we didn't have any money—and both of us were working outside the home.

My first real investment was in D'Arcy McManus & Masius stock, privately held, and interest rates were 19%. Some months the stock interest payments were larger than our mortgage payments! When we moved to the Twin Cities and I left DM&M, I had to sell my

DM&M stock. I turned around and bought Pepsi, Coke, Johnson & Johnson and Merck and started a regular savings program for our family. We didn't have a broker in the Twin Cities for a number of years. It was only on Gene's recommendation that we got a financial planner, and the rest is history. Twenty-two years later we are still using the same firm and individual who manages our stocks and bond holdings. Gerrie and I both sleep better at night, knowing he is managing our investments.

How have my other investments done? Real estate homes and lake property—terrific. For everything else—private companies and commercial real estate—I lost my shirt! Our planner advised against all of these "opportunities" as did my old boss, Gene. But I let friendship and loyalty trump sound business practices and common sense. Finding a good financial planner is not easy, but when you do, you'll find out as time goes by, this person will play a key role in your life, and he or she should ride up front with you in the first car of your train!

Lesson 2 – The Railroad Tracks
Caucasians vs. people of color are out of "the gate" first, or on a regular predictable schedule of professional development. Our "railroad tracks" are laid out for us. It's just a matter of how fast we want to go, or if we want to go at all. Yes, systemic racism exists, and there are far fewer trains for minorities in many cases! We still have a long way to go on that issue.

Lesson 3 – Kids Should Suffer Logical Consequences

My parents never sided with me when it came to teachers criticizing or saying I misbehaved. They were not "helicopter parents." If I got into a jam, it was my responsibility to figure out how to get out of it. That took some kind of patience, to be sure. Too many times today parents are critical of teachers and their assessment of their children. In looking back, the teachers I got to know and now thank, along with my parents, probably prevented me from not only going off the tracks, but crashing! Today teachers are expected to do everything, and if the kid screws up, it's the teacher's fault. The kid can't be wrong. The parents always take the side of the kid. Not in my generation! In those days, my parents said if I got in trouble, I'd better hope the police would get there first!

Lesson 4 – Equality of the Sexes

Equality/sexism…boys and girls…it's only natural to like or favor one child over another. Personalities and behaviors come into play so you have to work doubly hard at playing it down the middle but it's difficult. And the more children you have, the more difficult it is.

Lesson 5 – If Your School Isn't Doing a Good Job, Change Schools

Learning disabilities come in all shapes and forms. The key is for parents to recognize them early and address them. If your school isn't doing a good job with challenged students, change schools! You don't have very much time to mitigate the problem. I was lucky my mom was a teacher and a very patient parent.

Lesson 6 – Never Ask Someone to Do Something You Couldn't Do Yourself

I think today too many managers ask people to do things they wouldn't, couldn't or didn't have the courage to do themselves. And, more depressing, is the fact that if you work for someone like this, he or she doesn't support you when you make that difficult decision. Even worse, when he is criticized by his superiors for that action, he will throw you under the bus and deny he ever had anything to do with it.

   I learned this when I was in the Army in officer training from Sgt. Krizmarich and while on active duty from 1st Sgt. Dalrymple. In fact, on my discharge, the enlisted men and women hosted a party for Gerrie and me at Sgt. Dalrymple's home in South Carolina. He said in his 20-plus years in the Army, he had never hosted a party for a lieutenant. I honestly try to exhibit that behavior today. I realize I am not as physically able as I once was, but in the business and non-profit world, I tried to do that all the time. One of the many qualities I admired about my boss Gene in New York was he followed that principle in managing everyone who reported to him.

Lesson 7 – Always Hire People Who are Smarter than You Are

With regard to interviewing, hiring and firing, my best hiring story is I had just been made president of Kamstra and needed to hire a senior account manager. I knew of a former client who might be a great addition. I asked her to come in for an interview. She was seven or eight months pregnant. Mr. Kamstra, I am sure, thought I was nuts to hire this person, but we did. It turns out she was one of the best account people I have ever known and worked with.

Regarding hiring, Pat Fallon always knew the next person he was going to hire for his advertising agency. He was constantly on the search for talented people who would work hard and fit their culture. I used the same approach during my entire career. It took a lot of time, constantly interviewing, but pays off when you find the right person for the job. Hire slowly and fire quickly. Oh yes, "performance improvement plans," or, as they say, "probation" never worked. Ninety-five percent of the time you end up having to terminate the individual after which everyone comes to you and says, "Why did it take you so long to fire that person?" To which you never have a good answer.

Always hire people who are smarter than you are! I have tried to do that my entire career. Also never hire people who are just like yourself. I have always surrounded myself with those who have different personalities and backgrounds. And, most importantly, when someone comes up with a better idea, recognize them for what they've done. Never take credit for their ideas. That will result in a complete breakdown in trust with your co-workers and peers. No one will want to work with or for you.

Lesson 8 – Teachers Can Be Game Changers

If a teacher comes along and wants to spend time with your child, chances are he or she sees something in that child that you as a parent don't see, or you don't know how to draw out that trait or behavior and take it to the next level. Most teachers have the uncanny ability to do just that. There is no doubt in my mind looking back that I was on the road to becoming a juvenile delinquent if it hadn't been for Mr. Marsh. Two other teachers, Mr. Shirley and Mr. Jennings, were also supporting me during that difficult time and I am sure were talking with Mr. Marsh about how I was doing.

Lesson 9 – Choose Your Roommates. Don't Let Your Roommates Choose You

Roommates...roommates are an integral part of your development as a person. I think everyone should have one at some point in their lives. Let me tell you about John Conzemius. He was five years older than me and much smarter than I was. He had failed twice at college and now was determined to change that outcome. His dad owned a drug store in Council Bluffs, Iowa, and John had worked for him and for the local power company before coming to the University of Iowa. Like me, he was afraid of flunking out and getting drafted. This was during the Viet Nam war. He studied all the time, re-writing anything he submitted for our rhetoric class. That was when I really learned to study. I know in most cases you don't really have much choice about who your roommate is, but when possible, you should be the one to choose your roommate; don't let your roommate choose you. John deserves a lot of credit for my finishing college. Whenever I went out with my friends, he would be studying, so guilt became a big motivator for me to study.

Lesson 10 – Immerse Yourself!

John Conzemius, my college roommate, and I spent a summer in Guadalajara, Mexico studying Spanish. The Weavers, our host family, made it possible for us to travel all over Mexico and meet all kinds of people from all walks of life as we attended bullfights, operas, football games (soccer) and, my favorite, jai alai! I would encourage anyone, if the opportunity presents itself, to live in a foreign country for some period of time and learn the language. I guarantee two things: First, it will make you appreciate your home country more than you can imagine, and you will understand why everyone wants to come to America. Second, it will change you as a person regarding how you look at everything and will make you understand and appreciate other cultures if you take the time to engage in the culture of the country you are visiting.

Lesson 11 – Never Think You are Better Than Someone Else

Working in the meat packing house in the 60's was not easy, but all of a sudden, I was working with men and women who were less fortunate than I was. They wouldn't be going back to school in the fall. This was their career and livelihood. These were good people. They treated me no differently from anyone else, black or white. I felt right at home there and worked as hard as any one of them. I did this for two summers, Christmas break and spring break. Everyone was glad to see me come back, and I began to learn the importance of looking at people for who they are, not for what they do or what their status is in society. As my dad often said, "<u>Never</u> think you are better than someone else, and don't break your arm patting yourself on the back!" The lessons I learned working at the packing house affected me the rest of my ride on my train. The impact was phenomenal and a real motivator for me to finish college. On the other hand, I feel it's equally important not to forget your roots and from where you came or the people who were there for you along the way.

<u>Lesson 12 – Having a Bad Day</u>?
How many times have you heard someone say, "I'm having a bad day!" or perhaps you've said it yourself? It's something I never say because I think about that Army teletype and those families whose lives had been changed forever when they lost a son or daughter in the military. I lost two great high school friends, John Wall and Jon Winger, during the Viet Nam war. I can only imagine what their lives would have been like if they hadn't been killed.

<u>Lesson 13 – Hold Your Clients Close but Hold Competitors Closer</u>!
I find most clients know everything about their own products, pricing, and the benefits of using their product or service. So, whenever I was assigned a new account, I, of course, had "client input sessions" about their product, etc. But I immediately tried to learn everything I could about their competitors and what, if any, advantages we had over them. I was always surprised how little clients knew about their competition. Today with all the data, metrics and

benchmarks, I'm sure clients and companies will say, "We know what our competitors are doing!" All I can say is, that is a golden opportunity to make a real contribution to their business beyond advertising!

Lesson 14 – The Good, The Bad, and The Ugly

"Clients"—you hear that word a lot from lawyers especially, but most of the time it comes from organizations or businesses referring to the people they represent or for whom they provide services. A new term that has come into fashion is "guests." Retailers love this term. I just wish I felt like a "guest" in many of the stores I enter.

My first client was Jack Schutz. He was the advertising manager at Ideal Industries in Sycamore, Illinois. He knew from the "get-go" I did not know a lot about advertising, but, boy, was he patient with me. He had a very gentle manner about him and was always helping me become a "better account man." We became friends, but he and I always knew where "the line" was between our companies

Over my career, I have to admit, I have had some great clients. There are only two or three out of about 100 that I would never like to see again. The great ones with whom I remained friends after our formal business relationship ended—Roy Doering (Hurd Windows, now Sierra Pacific), Carl Cooper (Wagner Spray Painting), Jack Edl (Elkay Plumbing), Mike Brugh (Ergodyne and Toro), Greg Hammann (Nautilus and Levi), and John Cashmore (Weyerhauser).

Lesson 15 – Seize the Opportunity to Make Memories

We bought the cottage in 1973 for $18,000 from an 80-year-old widow, Clara Pathe. The house was built in 1931. Clara and her husband, a Chicago fire captain, had planned to retire there. However, he had a heart attack while fighting a fire and never got to live in that house. Even though the house was in pretty bad shape when we bought it, we learned that sometimes you just have to take a risk and hope that things work out. We still own that house today. It has been remodeled over the years while still maintaining the same footprint. We now spend spring, summer and fall there. In addition to having family and friends stay with us, I used it for business meetings and entertaining clients. Our friends, the Haags, announced their engagement during a visit and later built a home in northern Minnesota based on visiting our cottage and seeing how much we enjoyed it.

Lesson 16 – Night School Resumes Belong on the Top of the Pile

Prior to starting my M.B.A., I was working on Northwest Industries for whom we were doing their corporate advertising in 1976. I would meet with Dick Strubel, probably one of the most intelligent businessmen I have ever known. He knew my shortcomings and encouraged me to get my degree. Being a veteran, I was eligible for the G.I. Bill. I was also paid by DM&M for each course if I got a "B" or better plus my regular salary! I was admitted to Loyola, Northwestern, and the University of Chicago. I chose Loyola. There were only 14 courses, no thesis, and it had a downtown campus.

Initially, I was the only male in my classes. Illinois courts had ruled that business schools had been discriminating against women, and I was a veteran so they had to take me. It didn't start out well. The women hated my being in their classes. I knew the professors felt sorry for me, but it worked—two or three nights a week, up at 4:00 a.m., home by 10:00 p.m., saw my family in the morning, took four years!

Here's the key lesson: Whenever I would interview someone, I would ask them to tell me a little bit about their childhood, how they grew up, and their relationship with their parents. I've interviewed hundreds of people, and that has always been my way of finding out what kind of person he or she was. "I haven't spoken to my mother in 15 years," one CFO told me. She was a problem. Night school—for some reason I had always looked down on people who got their degrees at night...until I did it myself! Now those resumes go to the top of the pile.

When I got to Minneapolis, I taught at Metro State University in their evening M.B.A. program. For two years, I taught the capstone marketing course and introduction to Marketing. One student told me I had prevented her from dropping out once she heard I had failed statistics the first time. Love those students who go to school after they've worked a full day at another job! These are the true "rock stars" of the business world! But as teachers, we also need to be careful of what we say to students. It can affect a person for the rest of his or her life. Positively or negatively, just look how their remarks affected me throughout my life!

Lesson 17 – Career Choices...Never Act Alone

Gerrie and I made a choice to turn down a move and a promotion. This just wasn't done in those days! None of our friends could believe it. Many people, at some point in their careers, face this kind of decision, and it's especially tough in two-career families, because you never know until later if it was the right decision. My only advice if you're forced or given a choice to make a career change is to talk it through with one of your teachers or mentors in addition to your significant other. I did this with Dennis and with Wally. Parents or family are generally not good sounding boards because they've heard about only the bad points regarding your current situation and generally don't know the business you're in. Remember, my father thought I had a "pretend job!"

Lesson 18 – Leave Your Zip Code and Volunteer!

The Ad Fed was great. It allowed me to "leave my zip code" and meet other people who did what I did. I know it's more difficult today to find the time to do this. OK, how about a non-profit? Or a church group? Or the PTA? Any one of these organizations will allow you to develop a different perspective on what you do and challenge you to ask yourself, "Why am I doing what I'm doing?" If you have children, another option which is easier is getting involved with your kids and their activities. We joined Indian Princesses. It was for fathers and daughters, and it involved everything from making crafts to camping trips. On the camping trips, there were a minimum of rules—1. No pop before 8:00 a.m., 2. Only one can of pop at a time, and you had to finish it! There is no doubt in my mind these activities helped them develop their self-confidence, self-esteem and values. When our younger daughter, Karen, became a cheerleader, we hit the athletic circuit, and that group of girls was pretty tight. There were a lot of non-cheerleading activities. One in particular sticks out in my mind. Karen was invited to a weekend away at a fellow cheerleader's cabin. When Friday night came, after a game, she came home. I said, "What about the sleepover?" to which she replied, "I found out her parents weren't going to be there." Well, I guess so far as parents we did OK!

Lesson 19 – You Ain't Learnin' Nothin' When You're Talkin'!

Media representatives—In my career, I found these people to be some of the most fascinating people in the business. Initially I saw primarily business-to-business media representatives, but later it was broadcast representatives. Starting in Chicago, I saw Jack McGowan with "C.E.E." and Jim Mallon with "Forbes." Then in the Twin Cities it was Bob Bruley with "Business Week," Bill Wendling with "Engineering News Record" (I was the best man in his third wedding!), Dick Parsons with the "Wall Street Journal," and Ed Briner with "Remodeling" magazine, with whom I still stay in contact. These people are some of the best sales people I have ever known in my career. You know why? They first take the time to get to know you as a person—not your company, not your job, but you. Second, they are great listeners. I mean they excel at listening. Listening is probably the single-most important skill in business. In fact, the Army is where I first learned how important it is. I was actually forced to take a listening class at Ft. Jackson. There was a sign on President Lyndon Johnson's desk that said, "You ain't learnin' nothin' when you're talkin'!" I've never forgotten that. When there was a dispute of some kind, Gene Bartley, my most impactful and influential boss, would say, "Most situations are not black and white. The truth, in the majority of cases, is somewhere in the middle."

Lesson 20 – Look Before You Leap!
There are basically three types of boards: advisory boards and corporate boards, which can both serve in a public or private company, and non-profit boards. Each of them is very different from the others in their purpose and operating procedures. I have served on all of them.

Generally, the service terms are two to three years; however, a definitive term should be set and communicated to the members. Terms can be extended, but an Advisory Board needs fresh blood. All Advisory Board members need to sign a non-disclosure agreement since they will have access to the company's financial, legal and HR information. It is normal to provide members with a modest stipend plus reasonable expenses incurred for their participation in the board meetings. Any additional consulting the board member may do for the company should be a separate arrangement.

Each company will have a different expectation for their board members. It is very important if you agree to serve on a board to determine what is expected of you—everything from attendance to financial involvement and, most importantly, why they want you on the board and what they feel you can contribute to the growth and development of the organization. Non-profit boards are usually focused on raising money. They expect their board members to participate financially and use their "rolodexes" as a tool to help find others who will donate to the charities they support.

Lesson 21 – A Word About Agreements & Founders of Successful Companies

The biggest criticism I received from Gene in the first year of our relationship at True North was I was "too trusting" and, of course, he was right. I definitely made a very fundamental mistake when I did not engage an attorney before I signed a buyout agreement with Mr. Kamstra and all the other shareholders. I later learned that most of these earn-outs are for a three- or four-year period, not the seven or eight years I had agreed to. However, in all fairness, there is usually an up-front payment. Ours was probably not as large as most payments, but the company wasn't doing well when we got involved. If it weren't for John Cashmore, we would have had to lay off more people and close down the Austin office. It's funny that founders want you to be successful so they get their returns, but they don't want you to be too successful, which might make them look bad. One of my friends from Chicago and the Twin Cities ran into a similar situation and had the same kind of problems with the founder. He ended up leaving his company as well and under almost the same circumstances.

Lesson 22 – What's Next After High School?
If you've followed along on the train ride, you know the trouble I had figuring out my career path. But I am convinced of one thing: college or a 4-year degree isn't for everyone. Today there is way too much emphasis on getting those degrees! Look at the debt students are incurring when and if they finish! Crazy! I worked a lot of jobs to avoid incurring debt—roofing, retail, meatpacking, and, my favorite, as a bus boy.

I think everyone should work as a waitperson or in retail. I did, my wife did, and our two daughters did. I always empathize with people who have done that. When I interviewed job candidates, my second question was if they ever worked retail, etc. The answer told me a lot. Combining this information with their family backgrounds, I had a pretty good feel as to the type of person they were and what business and professional skills they possessed.

How do kids choose a college? Beats me! I have heard too many stories from parents to even have an opinion or give advice. I guess now you can hire a college search coach for that. All I can tell you, as our younger daughter, Karen, was looking at a variety of colleges, I asked her why she selected the University of Texas. Her reply was, "Diversity!" I rest my case.

Some of the most intelligent and well-adjusted people I know have never gone to college. This group includes Bill, who is my brother-in-law, Zach, Jim (all builder/remodelers), Ernie (our plumber), Jeremy (our electrician), Scott Spaeth (our butcher) and Dave Stanek a.k.a. That Tree Guy (our arborist). Another example is Bill Bounds, our former neighbor in Edina, who was a Green Beret and not intimidated by any person or situation. They are all successful businessmen who have a craft or skill that allows them to be successful, and I am proud to call them my friends. I am always impressed with their common sense and knowledge about how things work. In every instance, they have forgotten more than I will ever know about their craft. One in particular is Tom, our neighbor at the lake, who is a stone mason. His former employer called him "MacGyver." Remember that TV show about a detective who could figure out any crime? He is our neighborhood MacGyver and can figure out the solution to any practical problem. I would bet that any one of these individuals could fix anything in your home, and if they can't, call the Geek Squad! My dad always stressed, "Never think that you are better than the next person." And, finally, I learned this from a business associate later in life. He would say, "If I'm the smartest person in the room, you're in the wrong room!"

Lesson 23 – Beware of the "Dotted Line"
"Dotted Line" on a corporate organizational chart really means "broken line" in the business world. Beware when someone tells you that a certain employee has a "dotted Line" to you and what you're doing! In just about every case in which I was involved, it didn't work. I mean I was always the second person they listened to or took action from. Their boss was the

person who had the "solid line" or direct relation with them...period! OK, there are exceptions, but in the majority of cases, if you are the person who is assigned to the "dotted line" person, you will, nine times out of ten, be the secondary person for all decisions made plus attention and focus. Frankly, that is what P&L is all about. Or, as I like to say, there has to be "one throat to choke!" So, keep this in mind when someone says he or she has a dotted line to you. Chances are you'll never get your hands on that throat! Oh yes, the Army didn't have any "dotted lines" when I was on active duty, and I don't think they have any today!

Lesson 24 – Private Labels...Not So Bad After All
For years I trained my wife and daughters to buy only name-brand products. "No private label (generic) brands for us! Representing name brands paid my salary and sent you to college!" I would say. While staying in Florida every spring over the years, we would buy groceries at Publix stores and started sampling some of their private labels. Surprisingly, they were all outstanding products! Canned, frozen or baked, it didn't matter. This was a whole new world for me. During this past year because of the pandemic, we shopped only at Walmart and Costco for food. We couldn't live without Kirkland and Great Value products! Today unless you are Google, Amazon or Apple, you've got a tough road ahead of you building a brand—very difficult to do on the 2-inch phone screen of a potential customer.

Lesson 25 – Are You Being Fitted for Roller Skates?
I had never been fired before working for Gyro. But in hindsight, it was the right thing for them to do. I simply wasn't adding any value to their companies. I could see it coming, and I think most employees know when they're not contributing. If you're working today in a job and you can't discern if you're adding any value, you'd better take stock of yourself and figure out if there is a path to productivity before you are "fitted for roller skates" and sent out the door!

ABOUT THE AUTHOR

Dean Buresh grew up in the Cedar Rapids, Iowa, area. He received his B.A. and M.A. degrees from the University of Iowa, and completed his M.B.A. at Loyola University in Chicago. His entire career has been spent working in the advertising industry in Chicago, Minneapolis and New York. He now lives with his wife Gerrie at their lake home in rural northwest Wisconsin and serves on the boards of the Park Nicollet Foundation and the Brimmer Foundation.

www.ingramcontent.com/pod-product-compliance
Lightning Source LLC
Chambersburg PA
CBHW071523220526
45472CB00003B/1123